Principal Events i

	National and International	Regional
January	Russo-Finnish war. Leslie Hore-Belisha, War Minister, resigns from office. Butter, sugar, bacon and ham placed on ration. Waltham Abbey munitions factory explosion.	Snow and ice throughout the month, with rivers and harbours frozen and 31.9° of frost at Norwich. Influenza and measles epidemics. Heavy shipping losses off East Coast and German air attacks on lightships. First German bombers coast, sighted over Great Yarmouth and rural Suffolk.
February	Government announces new evacuation scheme for school-children. Navy rescues 299 British prisoners from German tanker *Altmark* in Norwegian waters.	Norfolk gives a lead with 38s. per week minimum wage for agricultural workers. Ploughing campaign resumed after freeze-up. Merchant ships armed and compulsory convoy system between Thames and Cromer Knoll. Debate on Sunday cinema opening.
March	Meat rationing introduced. Russo-Finnish peace treaty signed. Gas masks checked and fitted with new filters.	Many inhabitants leave east coast towns. Ploughing campaign at peak. Constant fighter patrols instituted over North Sea convoys.
April	Neville Chamberlain declares that "Hitler missed the bus". Germany invades Denmark and Norway. Budget increases income tax by sixpence to 7s.6d. and increases tobacco and alcohol taxes.	Invasion fears after German occupation of Denmark and Norway. German mine-laying plane shot down on to Clacton: two killed, 162 injured and 50 houses wrecked. Registration of billets for new schools evacuation scheme. Coastal resorts consider summer season prospects.
May	Norway surrenders. Germany invades Holland, Belgium Luxembourg and France; Low Countries occupied and French defeat at Sedan followed by German advance to Channel coast. Winston Churchill forms all-party coalition government and promises "blood, toil, tears and sweat". Local Defence Volunteers formed.	Invasion threat: troops posted along the beaches. Schoolchildren evacuated from east coast towns. First bombs on East Anglia, at Felixstowe. Queen Wilhelmina of the Netherlands and other Dutch dignitaries cross to Harwich. Bombers from East Anglian bases blast targets in Norway and Denmark.

EAST ANGLIA 1940

EAST ANGLIA 1940

by

R. DOUGLAS BROWN

TERENCE DALTON LIMITED

LAVENHAM . SUFFOLK

1981

Published by
TERENCE DALTON LIMITED

ISBN 0 86138 008 8

Text photoset in 11/12pt. Baskerville

Printed in Great Britain at
The Lavenham Press Limited, Lavenham, Suffolk

Contents

Publishers' Note

The publishers regret that the reproduction of certain illustrations is below the quality that they would normally demand. The *East Anglian Daily Times* and the *Eastern Daily Press*, who kindly permitted us the use of their files, were unfortunately unable to provide original photographs and, consequently, the pictures shown are reproductions from the printed newspapers. The same applies to those photographs acknowledged to the *Cambridge Evening News* that were so kindly provided by the Cambridge Collection of the Cambridgeshire Libraries. Where applicable, it was considered preferable to show illustrations, even if below our usual standard, rather than no pictures at all. This volume is the second of a series which will fully document the events in East Anglia, year by year, and we would welcome any photographs that apply to 1941 or subsequent years. These would be forwarded to the author for his use and, of course, returned in due course.

Index of Illustrations

Introduction and Acknowledgement

THE AUTHOR of a new history of the year 1940 must offer a good excuse, for already the number of books on this subject is countless. This was the most fateful year in Britain's long story, and the testimony of everyone who lived through it must be counted valuable historical evidence. I have tried to tell here the collective story of those who lived in East Anglia, that region of England which felt the threat of invasion to be most real and imminent in the weeks which followed the advance of German armed forces to the western shores of Europe. Neither the major historical works concerned with the whole sweep of strategy and action, nor the local monographs detailing the excitements of individual small communities, have been able to convey the flavour of everyday life on England's 1940 battle-front.

Insofar as I may have succeeded in doing so, I must thank many who have laboured in this field before me. I have set the East Anglian experience against the national and international scene, and for the general background I have been dependent on the various official histories of the war and such classic works as Sir Winston Churchill's *The Second World War*. It is only in recent years that much patient research has made available detailed information about the Battle of Britain in the air and I have used the already-published results of this research to piece together in a new way the story of the pilots who flew over East Anglia. Full acknowledgement of all sources will be found at the end of this book.

It is difficult to obtain accurate and balanced recollections of specific events which occurred over forty years ago and I decided, therefore, not to interview East Anglians still living who remember 1940. Instead, I have used diaries which were kept at the time. The assistance of a few individuals who have helped me in this is acknowledged elsewhere, and I wish to thank them. My principal source, however, was the Mass Observation Archive at the University of Sussex. There I was able to read the day-to-day experiences and impressions of more than a dozen diarists who lived in different parts of East Anglia, and I have quoted extensively from them. This material was supplemented by a number of reports prepared during 1940 by Mass Observation representatives who made special visits to the region to collect information. This East Anglian material in the Mass Observation Archive has not previously been published, and I am grateful to the Secretary of the Archive, Ms Dorothy Wainwright, B.A. for her assistance.

The daily newspapers published during 1940 in Norwich, Ipswich and Cambridge have been another principal source, and I wish to thank the Eastern Counties Newspaper Group Ltd and Cambridge Newspapers Ltd, and the editors of the various newspapers, for their valuable co-operation and for permission to quote from their reports and to reprint some of their photographs. I also acknowledge with thanks the co-operation of authors and publishers who have permitted me to quote short extracts from various books, as acknowledged in my "Notes on Sources".

I have made use of a number of primary sources, details of which are given elsewhere, and I wish to record my appreciation of the co-operation of staff at the Local Studies Department of the Norfolk County Library at Norwich, at the Cambridgeshire Local History Collection at Cambridge Central Library, at the Suffolk Record Office both at Ipswich and Bury St Edmunds, at the Local History Department of the Colchester Central Library, at the Reading Room of the Imperial War Museum in London, and at the Public Record Office at Kew.

During much of 1940 photography was forbidden in many areas of East Anglia, and consequently there are many aspects of war which cannot be portrayed here in pictures. The regional newspapers no longer possess negatives or original prints of the photographs they published and it has been necessary, therefore, to re-photograph from the pages of newspaper files, which inevitably involves some loss of quality. This defect, it is hoped, is more than compensated for by the value of a collection in more permanent form of a unique series of pictures.

R. DOUGLAS BROWN

Stoke-by-Clare, Suffolk
May 1981

CHAPTER ONE

A Time of Waiting

THE NEW YEAR crept whimpering from the shrivelled crysalis of the old, with no blush of health on its cheeks and no gleam of hope in its eyes. Britain had been at war for nearly four months. The words suggest drama, danger and the surge of adrenalin. The reality was a miasma of uncertainty, anxiety and frustration. In Western Europe there had been no set-piece clash of arms, not even a positive sign of movement by any army. No enemy bombers had attacked Britain, as had been predicted. No lists of casualties had been printed in the newspapers, as had been feared. No victories had been claimed, as had been hoped.

In Great Baddow, in Essex, a young man set down his feelings in his diary:

> "War talk has died down to a minimum in the last few weeks . . . One might not think that there is a war on at all . . . I am tired of the inactivity in almost every department of war. I would rather there was a big flare-up and get it all over with." [1]

This feeling was widespread. Rex Porter, living in lodgings in Chelmsford, felt exactly the same way. He was 23, just getting a firm foothold on the lower rungs of his chosen profession, but now feeling adrift as he waited to be called up for service in the army. The 21-year-olds had been called for training in 1939, the 22-year-olds were just registering and would go off in a few weeks, and then it would be the turn of his age-group. He was already feeling an identity with the men in khaki; when he went home to his parents at weekends he talked to as many of them as possible — the trains to Liverpool Street were packed with soldiers and after dark they were lit only by small blue bulbs which gave the dimmest glow, so that reading was impossible. As for the wider issues involved in the war, Rex had some doubts. What made it so difficult to reach conclusions was that he distrusted most of the war news in the papers; there was a Ministry of Information now but its principal function, he suspected, was to limit the flow of information. Whenever he visited London he bought copies of the American magazine *Life*; the United States was neutral in the war. But he also listened to the regular broadcasts from Hamburg Radio of a German propagandist who had been popularly dubbed "Lord Haw Haw". According to a B.B.C. enquiry in January, two listeners in every three sometimes tuned in to Haw Haw after listening to the 9 p.m. B.B.C. news bulletin, and so Lord Swinton was brought to the microphone in London to offer an authoritative British view of events. Rex Porter noted in his diary:

"At 9.15 p.m. we had the usual interlude. At the end of the news I said: 'Well, who shall we listen to, Swinton or Lord Haw Haw?' My landlady: 'Oh, not Swinton. I don't want to hear either of them, but I can't stick that old man.' But she did listen to the first part before going off to bed."

For most people the radio was the only form of amusement readily available during the winter months of early 1940. There was one comedy show full of catch-phrases which were already the common currency of the language. "TTFN," people called to one another as they parted, echoing Tommy Handley's abbreviated form of "Ta-ta for now". Handley played the role of Minister of Aggravation in Whitehall's "Office of Twerps". Jack Train played "Funf", the German spy who constantly rang up on the telephone — "This is Funf" cried countless small boys as they played. There was a civil servant called "Fusspot". ITMA, as the programme was called ("It's that man again"), exploded most of the more sombre preoccupations of daily life in irreverent laughter.

Pipes for the new organ in Norwich Cathedral in their permanent position in the triforium.
Eastern Daily Press

The B.B.C., however, was very conscious of its responsibilities. When the war began it broadcast only one programme, transmitted on two different wavelengths, and this ensured that everyone heard the many bulletins of official instructions and advice. In January 1940 it introduced a second programme intended for those in the armed services; as soon as there was a British Expeditionary Force in France, this Forces Programme began to teach "French for the troops". But the staple fare, of course, was music. The radio was the source of all the popular new tunes. It was interesting to note how the lyrics changed in different situations. Early in the war there had been the confident hit-songs like *There'll always be an England*, *We're going to hang out the washing on the Siegfried Line* and *Roll out the barrel*. Then there had been the wry humour of *Kiss me goodnight, sergeant major* and *Run rabbit run*. Now in January the new songs had a new tone; they included *Tomorrow is a lovely day*, *I shall be waiting* and *Faithful forever*. And Rex Porter, walking home to his lodgings one evening, came upon a company of marching troops who were singing *"When I get my civvy clothes on, Oh how happy I shall be"*.

The Mint working overtime, to cope with an increased demand for farthings caused by rationing and controlled prices.

Eastern Daily Press

The government was uneasily aware that things were not right. There had been a vast disorganisation of the ordinary routines of life. Schoolchildren had been rushed out of the big cities and deposited upon strangers in the countryside, and then had slowly drifted home again. Tens of thousands of men and women had volunteered for air raids precautions duties on the home front and then had found that they had nothing to do. The whole country had been plunged into a dusk to dawn blackout of almost paralysing intensity. On January 5th the Prime Minister, Mr Neville Chamberlain, delivered a speech which was specifically designed to repair sagging morale. But the people wanted action, not words. Rex Porter caught the mood in this diary entry:

> "A lot of searchlights can be seen this evening towards the south-east. So perhaps it's possible that the writing of this diary will be interrupted by an air raid alarm. We could do with a little bit and break the monotony." [2]

For most people the main impact of war was provided by the blackout. No slit or pinpoint of light must escape at any door or window; there was a constant stream of offenders before the local magistrates, most of whom had to pay fines of ten shillings* or one pound. It was unpleasant and sometimes dangerous to go out after dark, unless the moon was up. In a village near King's Lynn 18-year-old Jenny Carr went out to supper one evening in January with friends who lived a hundred yards away.

> "When I came out to come home I couldn't see an inch. It took me a long time to find the garden gate. My torch battery is in the last stages. I fell over the kerb three times and bumped the wall and fence four times. I thought I should never get home . . ." [3]

*The British currency of 1940 comprised pounds, shillings and pence, with twelve pence to a shilling and twenty shillings to a pound. The present metric penny is equivalent in face value (but not, of course, in purchasing power) to 2½ of the pennies of 1940. Many prices in 1940 were stated in guineas: a guinea was £1. 1s.

It was, in fact, now very difficult to buy torch batteries in the shops. Some traders dissected the large high-tension batteries intended for radio sets and offered for sale the individual cells, but this meant elaborate adaptation of the torch case, and the results were never good enough to justify the trouble. In any case, one had to be careful about using a torch at all. With a handkerchief wrapped over the glass, or red crepe paper stuck over it, and the torch pointed downwards, it might pass comment; but there were a number of prosecutions of those who flashed torches carelessly. The Chief Constable of Norwich issued a statement that it was not permissible to strike a match or to use a pocket lighter in the street during black-out.

Cars were allowed to use only one headlight and that had to be screened by an opaque mask in which only narrow slits or a small round hole could emit light. Even the destination signs or route numbers of buses were extinguished and passengers had to check with conductors where vehicles were going. The bumpers of vehicles and the "running boards" — the steps which ran along their sides under the doors — had to be painted white. Not surprisingly, road accidents were much more frequent in these conditions and so the government had imposed a 20 m.p.h. speed limit in built-up areas after dark.

There was considerable pressure for a relaxation of the restrictions, led by one of the national newspapers, and so, early in the year, it was announced that very limited lighting — and the amount was precisely defined — would be permitted for churches, restaurants and places of amusement, shop windows and markets and street stalls. Such lighting had to be immediately extinguished if a siren gave warning of air raid danger. On these terms, the government was even prepared to countenance a measure of street lighting: they called it "star lighting" because it was claimed that it gave the equivalent of the natural illumination of a bright starry night. A Norwich pedestrian was impressed:

> "After stumbling and feeling one's way along Colegate, the difference on emerging into Magdalen Street was especially noticeable. It was possible to walk along the path at a sharp pace without the aid of a torch." (4)

Norwich and Cambridge installed the special lamps, which gave one-fourhundredth of the illumination of a standard prewar lamp, in several streets and experimented for some months. Norwich City Council came to the conclusion, by a narrow majority of councillors and with its Chief Air Raids Warden dissenting, that the glow cast by the lighting would increase the danger of enemy air attack, and the lamps were removed. Cambridge decided the system was too expensive to instal throughout the town, but kept its artificial starlight in Peas Hill, Sidney Street and Drummer Street. The government decided that the best way to ameliorate the problems of the blackout was to introduce Summer Time prematurely — at the end of February — so that most people should at least get home before dark.*

---

*Summer Time was an "invention" of the first world war and thereafter was permanently adopted in peacetime, operating from April to October. After its forward extension to February in 1940, it operated continuously throughout the war years and was supplemented during the summers of 1941-5 by Double Summer Time (i.e. clocks were kept two hours in advance of Greenwich mean time).

Skating on Wroxham Broad during the cold weather. *Eastern Daily Press*

Early in 1940 the problems of getting about in the blackout were accentuated by exceptionally severe weather. It was the coldest spell East Anglia had known for 45 years. Norwich recorded 23.4 degrees of frost on January 3rd and 31.9 degrees of frost on January 20th, and for most of the month the ground was frozen a foot deep. Jenny Carr wrote in her diary:

"We walked along the beach. It is a most extraordinary sight, just like an Arctic scene. For about ten yards along the edge, the sea is frozen to a white hard snow in the waves. We talked to lots of people and none has ever known in memory it to have been like that before."

Jenny and her sister Bunty learned to skate for the first time. There was more skating than anyone had ever seen before. Wherever there was a stretch of ice there was a Bruegel-like scene of tiny muffled figures moving against a wide, white landscape. Although it was so cold, and the snows so deep that soldiers were being used to dig out trains buried on the tracks, yet on many January days the sun shone brightly. At Sandringham King George VI, the Queen and the Princesses Elizabeth and Margaret joined the skaters, and on Wroxham Broad one adventurer drove a motor-car over the frozen surface. Cambridge achieved its own special atmosphere with moonlight skating, and one energetic participant recorded afterwards that she had weaved and glided amid figures capped and gowned, but also including a turbanned Sikh and a uniformed policeman.

6

By the end of January in the villages, and a few weeks later in the towns, coal was in short supply. Bunty Carr recorded on February 2nd that:

"Coalman came, but could only let us have one sack and says he doesn't think there will be any next week." [5]

Rex Porter noted the situation in Chelmsford on February 21st:

"In this town coal supplies are almost at a standstill — we're carrying on partly with coke."

Even at the end of March the situation was acute. Bunty Carr spoke to a visitor who had a holiday home in Norfolk:

"A man from Cambridge who couldn't get any coal there told me he'd bought £5 worth at Heacham and was hiding it in his bungalow and would take a little home every time he came down."

There was much felling, sawing and stealing of timber from woodlands all over the region.

Culford schoolboys find lumbering a useful way to provide fuel.

East Anglian Daily Times

The bad weather continued into February, which was grey, damp and cold, with more snow about the middle of the month. There was a great deal of sickness. The Medical Officer of Health in Norwich estimated in January that one in ten of the city's population had influenza or severe colds. Nearly a quarter of the drivers and conductors employed by the Eastern Counties Omnibus Company in Norwich were absent sick one Monday morning. A

7

large proportion of the Army recruits at Gibraltar Barracks at Bury St Edmunds were reported on their backs with 'flu or German measles, and quite a lot of officers had pneumonia.[6] Throughout the first three months of the year influenza, German measles and pneumonia were endemic.

Fuels other than coal were erratic in supply. Bunty Carr's diary entry on March 14th was:

"Run out of petrol at the garage. Farmer out of paraffin — been unable to plough for two days. No coke for shop fire — none until June. Things seem very peculiar."

Private motoring had greatly declined. Only one person in ten owned a car and many car owners decided not to licence their vehicles at the beginning of 1940. At Norwich, for example, 7,757 vehicles were registered at the outbreak of war, but only 4,310 of these were relicensed in January, and most of those were commercial vehicles. There were experiments with gas-propelled vehicles, but there were not many of them. Rex Porter noted in February:

"This afternoon in Chelmsford market I saw my first gas-driven car, a big saloon looking as if it was carrying a baby barrage balloon on its roof."

The delays in ploughing caused by fuel shortage were more serious, for the frozen condition of the land had already set the farmers behind their schedules. Before the war began, but nonetheless belatedly, the government had announced a massive scheme to plough up grassland and to increase production of crops. War Agricultural Executive Committees had been set up to organise and supervise the operation, to provide tractors and additional labour where required, to prosecute farmers who refused to cooperate, and to check the fair distribution of the £2 per acre government grant. Norfolk had been asked to plough 27,000 additional acres in time for Spring sowing but, although the number of tractors in the county had increased to over 2,500, only 14,000 of these acres had been ploughed by mid-February. The Ministry of Agriculture, by then, was running a big advertising campaign to "Plough now — by day and night" and that is what East Anglian farmers did. Only 2,000 acres were ploughed in Norfolk between mid-February and mid-March, but after that the pace was frantic: nearly 5,000 acres in a fortnight, and the 25,000 acres target achieved by April 10th. There were many areas where ploughing was virtually impossible before the second half of February, but where targets were greatly exceeded before the time for sowing. By May 15th the overall situation was:

Norfolk, target 25,000 additional acres, had ploughed 37,150.
West Suffolk, 10,000 acres, had ploughed 15,809.
East Suffolk, 15,000 acres, had ploughed 17,188.
Cambridgeshire and the Isle of Ely, 12,000 acres, had ploughed 15,824.
Essex, 40,000 acres, had ploughed 26,939.

A Morris lorry fitted with a producer-gas plant demonstrated at Egerton's (Ipswich) Ltd.

East Anglian Daily Times

The government introduced a new Agriculture Bill in Parliament during January. It provided that War Agricultural Executive Committees might finance additional cultivation on behalf of farmers and recover the costs after the crops had been sold. It took account of the fact that more rye was being grown on light land newly turned from grass—this was especially so in Suffolk—and extended a guaranteed price to rye on the same basis as oats. It recognised that much land in East Anglia had drainage problems and gave Catchment Boards wider powers to improve minor water-courses, with grants of up to half the cost. By the time the Minister of Agriculture, Sir Reginald Dorman Smith, visited Norwich on January 27th the farmers who gathered in St Andrews Hall to meet him were in much better heart than they had been during 1939, when few of them had been able to make any sort of living from their land.

The agricultural workers were happier, too. The President of the National Union of Agricultural Workers, Mr E. G. Gooch, a Norfolk man, reported in January:

"The war has brought its difficulties, but it has not stopped the progress of the union, which is now periodically called into consultation at Whitehall and is being given the opportunity of playing its proper part in placing agriculture in a position to give the utmost assistance to the State in these days of war. Wages increases have been secured in all the counties."

Agriculture was a "reserved occupation"—its workers were not liable for call-up to the services. Their wage, at the beginning of 1940, was 36 shillings a week in Suffolk and slightly more elsewhere in the region. The union wanted £2. On February 12th the Norfolk County Agricultural Wages Committee resolved unanimously to give an increase of eighteen-pence to make a new minimum of 38 shillings for a forty-eight hours working week in winter and fifty hours in summer. The *Eastern Daily Press* commented: "Seldom can a wages settlement have been reached by negotiation that was more friendly."

9

Suffolk and Essex came into line soon afterwards and Cambridgeshire, which traditionally had paid rather more, raised their rate in April from 37 shillings to 39 shillings a week.

The labour force was now augmented by the Women's Land Army, which had been received in some areas initially with a degree of suspicion but which had proved its worth. "In the past few weeks farmers have had to alter their views and, instead of suspicion born of prejudice, we now find generous praise being given by a body of men who do not bestow it lightly," wrote the *Eastern Daily Press* in a leading article.

During the summer of 1939 the government had distributed to every home a leaflet which warned that "soon after the outbreak of a war . . . rationing would be applied to five foodstuffs—butcher's meat, bacon and ham, sugar, butter and margarine, and cooking fats." Ration books were distributed in November 1939 and everyone was required to register with a retailer. Rationing actually began on January 8th 1940, with each person allocated twelve ounces of sugar, four ounces of bacon and four ounces of butter a week. In the government's view, everything went very smoothly, but there were problems. Some customers went shopping without their ration books, which was a disaster if they had travelled into towns from the countryside, for the shop-keepers were required to be strict. Queues formed in shops while the unfamiliar coupons were clipped out with scissors. Some retailers suggested that a whole page of coupons should be deposited with them. Another suggestion was that pages should be perforated by putting them through a sewing machine.

The first day of official rationing in a Norwich provision store. *Eastern Daily Press*

Bunty Carr recorded in her diary in February a little local difficulty in her village:

"Two neighbours are having a row because a very poor family living in between them has let one of them have their butter ration and a pound of sugar. One wife was ill and the other went into her pantry for brandy and saw the butter and sugar right in front, with a tradesman's label that she knew they had not rationed with. Now every time they pass in the street one says loud remarks about the other."

The ideal of exactly equal shares for everyone was not achieved. There were some who could not afford to buy all their rations, and there were others who did not choose to. Jenny Carr noted:

"We have not had any bacon for about three weeks, as the last we bought was so salt and objectionable, as well as so dear — 2s. 2d. per 1lb. As for butter, we know some cows . . ."

Restaurants served only one lump of sugar with each cup of tea and butter was now served for the first time in small round pats. When organisations held annual dinners in hotels, only those who were seated at the top table were given butter with their rolls. At a British Legion new year's party in Essex when competitive games were played, one of the prizes was a pack of half a rasher of bacon, a lump of sugar and a small piece of butter.

The rationing of meat, originally intended to start in January, was postponed until March 11th. From that date every adult was entitled to 1s. 10d. worth (which meant, for example, one pound of pork chops), and children under six were allowed half of this amount. The delay enabled some of the problems to be smoothed out of the livestock control system which was introduced in mid-January. This ended all private slaughtering and created wholesale meat supply associations through which the Ministry of Food purchased all meat and livestock. The effects were profound. Twenty meat wholesalers in Norfolk and eight in Suffolk stopped trading on their own account and were swallowed up by the new organisation. Local markets almost collapsed; at King's Lynn on January 16th there were only 51 cattle, compared with a past average of 400 to 500, only 174 sheep instead of the customary 800, and only 171 pigs instead of the usual 800 to 1,000. But the consumer secured no benefit and many found themselves in a similar position to Jenny Carr in Norfolk:

"We have had no meat this week, as the butcher has not come. We had hardly any last week. A customer brought us two rabbits on Monday, so we're not starving, but lots of people have had no meat. Jimmy shot us two pigeons in the wood opposite."

11

But later, when meat had been on the ration for a month, she noted:

"We have not yet had to keep within our meat ration, having had at least 7s. 6d. worth a week for three people."

It was, indeed, a tall order to cut available meat supplies up into forty-five million equal rations, which was the number of consumers registered. Once things had settled down, country dwellers certainly fared much better than those in the towns. The latter could buy tripe, liver, hearts, kidneys and sweetbreads in addition to the basic meat ration, and also sausages and meat pies (although, as time passed, people began to suspect that there was not much meat in these); but the country folk could not only shoot rabbits and pigeons, but could keep and then slaughter a pig for home consumption, and most people kept chickens. One needed a permit to slaughter a pig and those who did so were expected to observe the rationed quantities and to detach and cancel the appropriate coupons in their ration books. This was described as a gentleman's agreement, and it may be that there were some who were not gentlemen. A bigger problem was that, in the early part of the year, there was a serious shortage of feeding stuffs, which led to the slaughter of many pigs and poultry. By April there were two million fewer pullets in Norfolk than a year earlier.

Some of the food issued on ration was unfamiliar to East Anglian customers. A Great Baddow diarist in lodgings there noted:

"Lard being unavailable, we have to use vegetable cooking fat. Mrs S. has not a very good opinion of it. 'It's no good for frying,' she said."

Home-killed meat was now largely replaced by Argentine and Empire frozen meat, but it was no cheaper, and there was general complaint. One of the Carr sisters was indignant:

"We tried some foreign meat for the first time and decided we would go without rather than eat that muck. The butcher is disgusted; he had never had any before, either. He has supplied and had meat from Sandringham and he had a splendid reputation."

The Ministry of Food tried to cheer people up with a doubling of the butter ration from March 25th, from four to eight ounces per person per week. They also announced that there was no immediate danger of tea, margarine or cheese having to be rationed. There was a general rise in food prices as the year passed, and a new problem for some people because traders would give no credit for rationed foods. Luxury foods had not disappeared, however, for in Norwich market in March there were pineapples at sixpence each, nectarines at threepence each and peaches at fourpence each, all from South Africa; cucumbers at one shilling, mushrooms at 2s. 6d. a pound, black grapes at

1s. 6d. a pound, Jaffa oranges at a penny and three-halfpence each, and bananas at five for sixpence. Chocolate was also still available, but that was soon to change for Caleys, one of the principal manufacturers, announced in January that sugar rationing required them to reduce their output by a third. Soon afterwards they suspended many of their 2,000 workers at the Chapel Field Works in Norwich.

There was one delicacy not to be found in markets. Thea Tregall, who lived in the Waveney valley in Suffolk noted:

"The boys have been out shooting blackies (blackbirds) round the corn stacks all day and have got lots. They all eat them in the village here. Johnny says they're very rich. He says sparrows are good, too, but you have to get so many to make a pie." [6]

The last open market at Norwich before the Government's Livestock Control Scheme became operative.

Eastern Daily Press

Some forms of clothing became difficult to obtain, or much more expensive, but there was no official rationing scheme at this stage of the war. Men could still buy, according to the advertisements, "a smart suit for three guineas". The Queen and the two princesses went to a January sale at Jermyn and Sons, a department store in the High Street in Kings Lynn, and bought silk scarves at one shilling each. Perhaps it was a sign of the times that their other purchases included overalls, as well as silk stockings. But when Jenny Carr went to buy herself a pair of lisle stockings in April she found:

13

SPRING IS JUST ROUND THE CORNER

IRIS is wearing one of Bonds' New Suits in fine quality West of England Cloth. There are several similar styles in some very attractive shades. Suits which are so essentially right for Town or Country, at .. .. **4 Gns.**

Bonds NORWICH

Spring fashions from Bonds of Norwich.

Eastern Daily Press

Popular records of the time including such titles as *My Heart Belongs to Daddy* and *God Bless You, Mr. Chamberlain.* ▶ *Eastern Daily Press*

"One shop no lisle and only very few silk and those over 2s. 11d. 'It's a job to get any now.' Went to the other shop: 'We haven't any nice lisle, only these, and they're very clumsy. They can't make them properly in this country. Those you usually buy are made in Germany, so there won't be any more.' I came home and took off my stockings altogether in the national interest, to save shipping and imports!"

People were only slowly getting used to the idea that many familiar things would soon be unobtainable. The Great Baddow diarist, who worked in a draper's shop, made this entry in early March:

"Underwear, whether woollen or cotton, is especially hard to get. But when customers are told that we have none of a certain article in stock, they look at you as though you are telling them lies."

At that time, too, a Cambridge mother was shocked when she took her son to buy him new shoes — "9s. 6d. a pair for a child not yet 2½ seems a big price to pay".

Wages and salaries began to move up a little, but East Anglia held to its pre-war pattern of lower earnings than in most other parts of Britain. When Lowestoft Town Council introduced "cost of living bonuses" for its white-collar employees its decision was that "where the annual remuneration does not exceed £275 there will be a 6 per cent bonus on the first £150, plus 3 per cent on the salary above that amount." The Corporation's manual workers' claim had already been met with a flat increase of three shillings a week. There was still a lot of unemployment — five hundred signed on regularly at the Labour Exchange in a small town like Hunstanton — but the total was falling as men were called up or drawn into the defence industries. There were not many of these in East Anglia, but Norwich and Ipswich had important engineering works and Garretts at Leiston was so busy turning out armaments that it had to introduce shift work. The shipbuilding yards along the coast, particularly at Lowestoft, were overwhelmed with work. The Norwich footwear industry, with 9,000 operatives, was also working flat out; it had some government work, but most of that had gone to the Midlands and Norwich was free to concentrate on "utility" footwear for the civilian population, to replace the dainty styles it had been selling a year earlier.

Pensioners formed a minority facing economic hardship and their claims were pressed in Parliament, but the Chancellor of the Exchequer firmly rejected a proposal that the ten shillings a week pension should be increased to fifteen shillings. He promised instead a supplementary pension payable in cases of proven need, but there would be a household means test and sons and daughters living with aged parents would be expected to contribute.

The new offices of the Melford Rural District Council in Newton Road, Sudbury.

East Anglian Daily Times

Some people, traders in particular, became worried about deteriorating services; the Post Office was a favourite target. At the January meeting of the Downham Market Urban District Council it was said that "the first delivery of letters in the town was often as late as 9.30 a.m. There was no mid-morning delivery and not always one in the afternoon." One councillor complained: "We tradesmen suffer great inconvenience. I myself have had important orders come by post too late to despatch by the early buses." Bunty Carr, whose family kept a village shop, offered confirmation in her diary:

> "Takes three or four days now to order things. Before the war we always posted our letters on the 9 p.m. bus — it was one of the social occasions in the village. I could order things from Norwich then and get them the next day by carrier, or from Ely by the first morning train. I never expect anything now within four days."

Before the war there had also been three commercial travellers calling every day, to see that stocks were kept up; by the Spring of 1940 the visitors were down to three a week.

Leisure activities were similarly reduced, but brave efforts were made to keep alive sports activities, the cinema and theatre and the various voluntary organisations.

Football had a hard time. Ipswich Football Club suspended indefinitely all activity as soon as the war began. Other clubs fixed what friendly games they could. Colchester United gave up the struggle during January and

16

suspended play for the rest of the season. Norwich City persisted with what were termed regional matches, but crowds were tiny. When they played Southend in February and lost 3—0, there were only 500 spectators. Along the coast the yacht clubs planned a programme for the coming season, but not everyone was optimistic about the prospects. The *Eastern Daily Press* did its best to provide encouragement:

> "Sports clubs, for whom the future looked so bleak half a year ago, are meeting to decide how they shall go forward this season . . . There is a quiet determination not to let the war stop the run of the ball, either on bowling green, cricket pitch or lawn tennis court. It is a healthy sign."

Certainly the various organisations, sporting and otherwise, kept up the tradition of their annual dinners. Cromer Fire Brigade, sitting down to its annual dinner at the Red Lion Hotel, had their full war kits close at hand and the fire engine parked in the hotel yard. But when the officers of the Essex County Council held their annual dinner in the Shirehall ballroom at Chelmsford, two-thirds of the men were in dinner jackets and some in tails.

The Suffolk public schoolboys (in coloured shirts) and the Norfolk public schoolboys photographed before the game at the Ipswich R.U.F.C. ground. The Suffolk schoolboys won by 14 points to 11.

East Anglian Daily Times

The year began with the customary pantomimes: *Cinderalla* at the Arts Theatre in Cambridge and at the Hippodrome in Norwich, *Mother Goose* at the Norwich Theatre Royal. In Colchester the local Repertory Company presented Terence Rattigan's comedy *French without tears* in the Albert Hall. The Maddermarket Theatre, the special pride of Norwich, kept going, presenting plays for one week in each month, choosing the time of the full moon. Nugent Monck, its director and now an air raid warden as well, saw the theatre as a means of escape from the war. All military plays were out, he declared. "*Coriolanus* and *Julius Caesar*, both are dictator plays and I shall not do them." He could never plan for more than a few weeks ahead, for about half of his Norwich Players were by this time in the Services or on government duties, or soon were likely to be. In January he presented a play by a 17th century Japanese dramatist, Chikamatsu, and soon afterwards his choice was Strindberg's play *Easter*.

The theatre made headlines in unusual ways. When, after an interval, plays were resumed at the Norwich Theatre Royal, the first production was a melodrama *Gaslight*, with Winston Churchill's daughter, Sarah, in the lead role. The ladies of Norwich's knitting circles presented her with a scarf for her father. During 1939 the Theatre Royal had been leased to the impressario Prince Littler, but now it passed back to Jack Gladwin, whose career in theatrical management in Norwich stretched back to 1926. He opened again on April 1st with a revue called *Tropical Express*.

But the show that really attracted attention, of an unwelcome kind, was an all-female revue, *Meet the Girls* presented at the Norwich Hippodrome in February. The Chief Constable of Norwich launched a series of prosecutions in respect of several of the sketches in the programme. Their titles, *Food Control*, *ARP* Warden* and *AFS*, echoed the bleak themes of everyday life and the evidence as reported in the local press gave no indication to the contrary. But we must conclude that they had a style and content that was altogether more exotic, for the four actresses who performed in them were each fined £1. We may get a clue from the text of a letter read in court which had been written by a former manager of the theatre to one of his associates:

> "We have been having a great deal of trouble during the past few weeks with the Watch Committee in Norwich, as regards the shows which have been presented at the Hippodrome. Being a cathedral city, they are naturally very strict, but just lately they have got worse than ever and I should think they are the strictest in the country. They will not tolerate any 'blue' gags or vulgarity of any kind whatever . . ."

What effect this case had on the character of later shows has not been recorded, but it did not discourage titillation in the titles, for in July the Hippodrome was presenting *Strip Please*.

*A.R.P. – Air Raid Precaution   A.F.S. – Auxiliary Fire Service

Sarah Churchill receiving a scarf knitted by the Norwich Women Liberals for her father, Winston Churchill.

Eastern Daily Press

Apart from the radio, the cinema was still the most popular form of entertainment. Those who did not like the blackout went to afternoon matinée performances. Early in the year a movement began to have cinemas opened on Sundays, for the benefit of servicemen, but the idea was extremely controversial and many local authorities were loath to sanction it. Before 1940 was out, however, practically every town with a cinema had capitulated. Rex Porter noted in his diary a conversation between a Chelmsford councillor who had voted for Sunday cinemas — Chelmsford was one of the first towns to permit them — and a member of his staff:

> "Councillor X said: 'A lot of girls in this town are being ruined and that will keep going on if the chaps haven't got anything else to think about. I see plenty of it going on'. (His house overlooks one of the local parks). Y, 31, married, quiet and sober type, commented: 'The worst of this is there'll be Sunday cinemas after the war, too. They'll find it impossible to stop them again now they've started. I like the Sunday to be kept quiet.'"

The dance-halls were also very much in business. In Cambridge, for example, there were dances every evening at the Rex Ballroom and regular Saturday evening dinner-dances at the University Arms Hotel. At many events, women were far more numerous than men and they danced together. Quicksteps were the most popular, but the palais glide, the Lambeth Walk and the boomps-a-daisy were included at most dances. An attempt was made at Chelmsford to introduce a new dance called the Blackout Stroll, but it was a flop.

19

A gift of clothing for evacuees sent from Canada, being sorted by members of the Cambridge W.V.S.

Cambridge Evening News

With these various amusements people tried to cushion themselves against the inconveniences and frustrations. Sometimes they almost forgot the war. A Mass Observation "Suffolk Village Report" prepared in April asserted:

> "The war does not seem to have affected the life of the people in the villages round here as much as might have been expected. There has been an intensification of agricultural activity and gardening . . . There is perhaps less interest in the newspapers and in the wireless than in towns . . . Conversation does not come round to war topics of its own accord." [7]

The rise in prices, the call-ups and the billetting of soldiers in the neighbourhood were the only war subjects that were widely discussed, according to this report. There was little sign in most areas at this time of an informed public opinion about war aims and war strategy. Bunty Carr noted this experience in her Norfolk village:

> "I went to see the cobbler and find he has a map of Europe pinned in the shop. He tells me that people come in and look at it and say 'Well, I didn't know Poland was *there* before. However did our government think they were going to help them?' He says there are very few in the village who know where the countries of Europe are situated . . ."

More sophisticated folk did not necessarily weigh the circumstances of the time with any greater intelligence. The Cambridge Union, at its debate in February, spent the evening discussing the proposition "that Hitler is the Devil and Stalin his Chief Stoker". And in Chelmsford Rex Porter overheard a private conversation in which a local magistrate was speaking of "Mussolini and his macaroni dagoes". By this time the word "Huns" was coming increasingly into use.

The Prime Minister, Mr Neville Chamberlain, complete with umbrella, on his 71st birthday.

B.B.C. Hulton Picture Library

There was one solace for country people, age-old but undiminished in its effect upon the human spirit. The drear winter was passing, the sap was rising and, even before February was out, Nature was dramatically signalling the prospect of a brighter future. Jenny Carr caught the atmosphere in this diary entry:

"Quite Spring-like and sunny. Snow all gone and crocuses and tulips have shot up under it. Lovely country noises of birds singing, threshing and sawing. Even the tortoise is awake. The worst of it is Mother is talking of Spring-cleaning."

These sentiments were echoed by another young lady diarist, Thea Tregall, as she observed the progress of the seasons at the other end of East Anglia, in the Waveney Valley:

"There was a fine high wind blowing and the sun and the blue Spring sky and the aconites taller and more open than they have ever been before, and snowdrops and crocuses, but all so clear at the edges, so much too distinct to be real."

This stirring of the blood was evident even in old men's veins. Neville Chamberlain, Prime Minister and war leader, went to the Central Hall at Westminster early in April and told a conference of Conservative Party activists: "I want to say to you now that after seven months of war I feel ten times as confident of victory as I did at the beginning . . . One thing is certain: Hitler missed the bus."

CHAPTER TWO

Responsible Authority

IN A spacious house known as "St Regis", in Montague Road in Cambridge, an embryonic Government of East Anglia had been set up*. It was headed by a 58-year-old Scotsman, Sir Will Spens, who had distinguished himself during the inter-war years as civil servant, academic, theologian and administrator. He had been the Master of Corpus Christi College for fourteen years and during 1931-3 he had served as Vice-Chancellor of the University. His outstanding reputation fitted him, in the government's view, for one among a group of appointments which were the most remarkable ever made in British public life.

If Britain had been invaded and if the German forces had isolated the eastern counties from the government in Whitehall, then Sir Will would have taken complete and absolute power to govern East Anglia as he saw fit. The government had divided the country into a number of regions, of which East Anglia was one, and each had been placed in the charge of a Regional Commissioner. Sir Will and the others were summoned to Whitehall to be briefed well before the war began. The Lord Privy Seal, Sir John Anderson, explained to them that in an "extremity" they would be expected to take the "full powers of civil government". They were being given, he said, a "dormant commision" from the government which would become active under circumstances of which they themselves would be the judges. If that happened, they would be indemnified for every action they took, provided it was performed in good faith. [1]

The Eastern Regional Commissioner's area stretched from the Wash southward to the Thames estuary and the outskirts of London, and westward as far as Bedford. Obviously, with so large an area and so heavy a responsibility, a strong organisation needed to be brought together and tuned to the pitch at which it would be effective to tackle any emergency. "St Regis" became a hive of activity. One of the most influential and experienced members of the East Suffolk County Council, the Earl of Cranbrook, became Deputy Regional Commissioner and a senior civil servant moved in as Assistant Regional Commissioner. Many of the most important government departments, including the Ministry of Agriculture, the Ministry of Information and MI5, had by early 1940 installed their representatives at the Cambridge regional headquarters. A "war room" was set up there, linked by telephone

---

*The part of Montague Road in which "St Regis" stands was renamed Hamilton Road in 1967. The house is now occupied by the Social Services Department of the Cambridge County Council.

and teleprinter land lines with Whitehall, and communications staff were recruited from the Post Office. The other necessary staff was largely provided by the civil service, but Sir Will was also able to obtain the services of a number of university dons. [2]

This organisation created, the government decreed that in "normal" war conditions it would limit its responsibility to coordination of the activities of all the various decision-making and executive bodies in the region. It would keep contact with the local authorities, with the A.R.P. organisation, the fire service and the police, and with the armed services stationed in East Anglia. It would endeavour to smooth away any problems which arose between them, using diplomacy and personal persuasion alone. In practice, Sir Will Spens seems personally to have maintained a close contact with the senior Army officer in the region, the Commander of the II Corps, Lieut. General H.R.S. Massy, the Earl of Cranbrook made it his special responsibility to liaise with the local authorities, and the Assistant Regional Commissioner kept in touch with his colleagues in the civil service. From time to time meetings were called at "St Regis" in Cambridge and these were normally attended by a Military Liaison Officer, an H.M. Inspector of Constabulary and Chief Constables of the various police forces in the region. [3]

The Regional Commissioner, Sir Will Spens, giving a formal send-off at Cambridge of the first Y.M.C.A. mobile tea car.

Eastern Daily Press

Lieut. General H. R. S. Massy (second from left), Commander of II Corps in East Anglia, seen with staff officers in the Operations Room at his H.Q.   *Imperial War Museum*

Local government was subjected to enormous stress in the transformation to wartime organisation. Many of the customary activities were now circumscribed; there was, for example, a Treasury ban on all new capital works, although this was relaxed in a few special cases, as when the Board of Education approved the completion of new schools which had been started before the war at Earlham and Stalham, in Norfolk. On the other hand, air raid precautions, evacuation and the drive to increase food production on the farms had burdened them with heavy new responsibilities. At the same time that the Regional Controller was appointed, the Ministry of Home Security had requested each local authority to nominate an A.R.P. Controller — "some one person who is empowered to take immediate executive action" over any aspect of civil defence. Councils, it was suggested, might choose one of their own chief officers, or the local chief police officer, and any other such local person who would inspire confidence. [4]

The Ministry of Home Security, from the outbreak of war, passed its information and instructions to these Controllers. If necessary, in extreme conditions, they could act at once. When the system was first devised, before the war, it was expected that conditions would be such that the local authorities would have to delegate their powers to small Emergency Committees and these, it was suggested, would serve as "half-links" in the chain of command from the Ministry of Home Security in Whitehall to the A.R.P. Controllers in the localities. The Ministry would deal with the Controllers, who would report their instructions to the Emergency Committees for discussion before they were acted upon. In a crisis, the Controllers would act first and report afterwards.

When the war began, most councils appointed such Emergency Committees and left most of the detailed decision-making in their hands, and in a few places, of which Harwich was an example, this sytem, or something like it, was retained throughout 1940. But the more general rule was that, once it was appreciated that normal routines need not be disturbed by the war, Councils quickly re-asserted their authority and functioned as in peacetime. There was one concession to the times: normal elections to councils were suspended for the duration and if a vacancy occurred the sitting councillors nominated someone to fill it.

The A.R.P. services had a backbone of full-time professionals, and a large number of volunteer part-timers. The professionals wore blue cotton uniforms and were issued with steel helmets and gasmasks which were superior to the civilian issue. A.R.P. helmets were painted black with white lettering to indicate the branch of the service: Warden, Rescue, Casualty or Decontamination service. Part-timers had to make do with a simple arm-band until well into 1940. The vehicles required for these services were secured mainly by voluntary arrangements with private owners; the Ministry authorised the purchase of second-hand cars for the Rescue and First Aid parties — provided they did not cost more than £30 each.

Practice by the members of No. 1 First Aid Party A.R.P. at Shirley School, Cambridge.

Cambridge Evening News

The trouble, as 1940 began, was that there was no real work for the A.R.P. services to perform. Those who were being paid were subjected to some criticism. When Norwich opened an A.R.P. Services Social Club on January 1st, with a billiards room, games room, reading room and bar, there was public criticism that the ratepayers' money should not have been spent in this way. In Chelmsford Rex Porter spoke to a Council manual worker:

"This A.R.P. — biggest bloody waste of public money that ever was. Look at that (pointing to the Shire Hall wardens' post) — £15 a week that costs the ratepayers. Five wardens there are, someone's on day and night. Nothing to do but sit on their arses. I don't suppose the phone's rung more'n three times since the war began. They're too bloody lazy to even sweep their own room out."

As the result of an investigation ordered by the government early in the year, the A.R.P. service was reorganised after April. The number of whole-timers was drastically reduced: even in what were regarded as the chief target areas, there were to be only two at each post. The paid staff in the Report and Control Centres were also cut back, and the Home Secretary appealed for more part-time volunteers to ensure that the efficiency of A.R.P. was not reduced. There was a new emphasis on intensive training. [5]

The government had distributed 35 million civilian gasmasks during 1938-39. In March 1940 a general appeal went out that they should be produced at warden's posts to be checked and repaired if necessary. At about the same time the government heard that the Germans had a new gas which could be used in aerial bombardment and against which the existing gasmask offered no protection. So new filters were ordered and by May wardens were beginning to fit these as extensions to the standard gasmasks. [6] An additional responsibility during the early months of 1940 was the fitting of special respirators for small children. These were of two kinds. Small babies were provided with a "Protective helmet" which completely encapsulated them, and into which mothers would have had to pump air using a special bellows attachment. Children from two to about 4½ years of age had another type of respirator which was popularly known as a "Mickey Mouse".

When the supply of children's respirators arrived in the Waveney Valley early in March Thea Tregall volunteered to help with the fitting. The village hall was booked for an afternoon "demonstration meeting" and, as well as the mothers and children, three wardens and a first aid worker turned up. Here is Thea's description of what happened:

"At 4 p.m. the mothers began to arrive for the baby masks to be fitted. Mr D., a warden, kept telling the mothers that they musn't put the children in except when gas was there — 'only actually when the gas is turned on'.

We had no trouble with the babies, though Mrs B's, which is nearly too big at one year and two months to get into the bag, kicked rather, and she says if she ever has to put him in, he'll kick it to pieces in no time.

The small children just wouldn't go into the Mickey Mouses. They all howled. We got two in, rather brutally, but they wept for relief when they got out again. So the mothers signed for them and took them home, to be got used to."

Alternative means of transport due to petrol restrictions — a low gig photographed at Wroxham.

Eastern Daily Press

There were still large numbers of mothers and children in East Anglia who had been evacuated from London in September 1939, despite a mass movement back to the capital during the winter. An official count at January 8th established that about half the school-children had returned home, and about nine out of every ten of the mothers who had been evacuated. Most parts of East Anglia scored better than the national average. In Norfolk there were still 11,079, or over 63 per cent, of the original evacuees; in East Suffolk there were 9,765, over 48 per cent; in West Suffolk, 2,629, over 56 per cent; in Cambridgeshire, 4,167, well over 60 per cent; and in the Isle of Ely, 3,549, which was over 62 per cent. It had been a traumatic experience for all concerned: the children, their parents and teachers, the families on whom they had been billetted — and even for the officials who had carried through the planning and execution of the scheme. The War Cabinet, weighing the experience, resolved that never again would they attempt a mass evacuation at speed. At the same time, they remained convinced that if air raids began, as they considered they must do, young children must be removed from target areas. A new evacuation scheme was, therefore, announced in February.

Parents were asked to register the names of children they would wish to be evacuated if and when air raids began. These children could then be medically examined and monitored until the time came to move them. No mothers would accompany them this time. This, it was believed, would eliminate most of the difficulties experienced in 1939 and so house-holders in the reception areas, which included East Anglia, were now asked to put their names on to a register of those who pledged to provide accommodation when the expected emergency arose. [7]

Throughout March and April the government kept up a massive propaganda campaign, which included a letter from the Minister of Health to householders in East Anglia pleading for their support. Rex Porter's landlady listened to a broadcast appeal and then remarked: "I'd rather have forty soldiers than two of those children". And that, it seemed, was the general view, for the Billeting Officer in Chelmsford received only 160 offers of accommodation in response to the 10,000 appeal letters he distributed. "You have to go round door to door and beg people to take them," he said.

Without waiting to know the response, the Ministry of Health allocated the likely evacuees to the various districts, and a number of them promptly lodged their claims to be excused. Southwold, which had been allocated 300 children, suggested to the Ministry in April that they did not consider the East Coast to be safe enough to be a reception area. This argument was rather weakened by the town council's additional point that the boarding-house keepers wished to keep accommodation vacant for the summer visitors they hoped to welcome. Of the 923 forms distributed in Southwold, only 23 were returned with offers of help. Marshland Rural District Council made representations to the Ministry that it should not receive more evacuees because so many of the women in that area worked on the land that a diversion of their attention would seriously affect food production. In response to the 4,800 forms distributed there, only 250 offers of help were received. The Ministry allocated 800 children to the area, notwithstanding.

These statistics do less than justice to the people of East Anglia. In one area of Suffolk to which 2,000 children were allocated, the initial distribution brought in only 247 offers of accommodation. A house-to-house canvass was then tried and the final conclusion was that at least 1,500 children would be accepted voluntarily when the need actually arose. Although there was a general reluctance to make forward commitments, there was unlimited goodwill towards children once they had arrived in a community. Thea Tregall lived with her parents in "the big house" in her Suffolk village and, voluntarily and entirely unofficially, she gave a great deal of time to the amusement and instruction of the evacuees who had come there. That she established a close *rapport* with them is clear from this extract from her diary during April:

"A marvellously fine day. Daddy and I took the boat up to the boathouse and sat there and read. The willows are beginning to shoot now, a sort of faint green haze over them from a distance. In the afternoon, Daddy sat in the rose garden and I let Doosny and Wif and Ben and a lot of the younger ones go in the boat.

I sat on the lawn and meant to do some mending, but Sharper climbed over the fence and came in and talked about birds, so we went round the nests and saw that two blackbirds and a mavis were sitting, and so didn't disturb them. I gave him an egg from the deserted nest that was too near the kitchen door, and I think he'll be able to blow it.

Took him up on the roof to see if we could see anything and there was a tree-creeper going up and down the pine tree, with its mouth full of moss. Sharper was very excited and told the others: Johnny, Joe, Mart and Eric, who had been getting sacks of greenstuff for Eric's rabbits.

Joe said there was a fieldfare's nest in the fir tree on the Piece, and I went to look, as I've never heard of fieldfares nesting here; it was a largish, tidy nest high up; couldn't see the bird well, as she flew before I came to it, but she looked like a large thrush. Perhaps only a missel thrush. Hart's dog came through the hedge and he and Diccon had a most unholy fight. Did some mending of stockings, and alterations to a hat I loathe."

It is a remarkable evocation of a Spring afternoon in the country, and the London evacuees bring to it an extra dimension of pleasure.

February threshing on a farm near Norwich. *Eastern Daily Press*

Of course, it was not always as peaceful as that, even in these early months of the year. On most days, there were aircraft overhead, during most nights the beams of searchlights criss-crossed the skies. This activity was evidence of the substantial presence in East Anglia of the Royal Air Force and its associated anti-aircraft defences. The planes that roared overhead could usually be counted friendly. The Carr sisters' diaries are full of references to Blenheim bombers hedge-hopping over the Norfolk marshes and Rex Porter, who was a keen student of aviation matters, noted the flights of Hurricanes, Spitfires and Blenheims over Chelmsford. Occasionally, however, those who lived near the coast saw something more ominous, as did Bunty Carr on February 23rd:

> "I was at home alone this afternoon and went out into the garden a minute, heard an aeroplane, and realised a German plane was above me, flying very low and quite slowly, a very big variety.
>
> I felt quite pleased with myself. It appeared to have come from the sea, over the marshes, turned over our lawn, and circled back towards the North Sea. I saw two women with shopping baskets and the postman and a shopkeeper had recognised it, but they stood out in the road to see if there was any further fun. Everyone I told wished they could see it . . ."

The absence of a sense of fear in this diary entry is matched when crashes of R.A.F. planes near villages are reported. There were plenty of them. The authorities moved quickly to place armed guards on them and to keep away the public, but the local inhabitants were usually on the scene within minutes. When a plane came down near the Carr sisters' village on March 7th, Jenny was off like a shot:

The front of the Grand Hotel, Lowestoft, with windows blown out by the explosion of a mine against the sea wall.

Eastern Daily Press

"We cycled down the lane to the nearest point to the plane and walked ever so far across marshland and it still seemed in the distance. An Army officer and a private were following behind and caught us up and asked if they were going the right way to the plane. We said we thought so, and walked the rest of the way across planks over creeks and bogs to the plane.

Two airmen were sitting on the wings and two women were just arriving with a pot of tea, cups and saucers, a tin of milk, sandwiches and cakes for the airmen. Five grammar school boys and about seven other small boys and girls were rushing around the plane, climbing on the wings and peeping inside."

The following day Bunty Carr added a postscript:

"Hear there is a raging discussion in the village about who reached the aeroplane first. Local excitement very great . . . As few of the inhabitants have ever seen a battleship or any Army equipment, the R.A.F. is the only service that seems real and definite."

Younger people were extremely interested in the more technical aspects of the war. At Chelmsford, as Rex Porter observed, the magazine room of the local library was invaded at 4 p.m. each day by boys from the grammar school, who then monopolised such publications as *Flight*, *Aeroplane* and the *Illustrated London News* — "anything which presents the war in the technical-mechanical manner which so appeals to the modern boy; they sit at the tables in pairs and eagerly point at pictures of Spitfires and battleships."

It was the towns and communities along the East Coast for whom the war piled up problems most quickly and seriously. Their prosperity depended in large measure on the holiday trade; but could they expect to attract *any* visitors in this summer of 1940? They tried to remain optimistic, despite some unhelpful publicity. During January, Lowestoft was badly shaken up by a drifting mine which exploded against the sea wall; that was inevitably reported, for debris was scattered in the main streets, bathing chalets were smashed, and the Grand Hotel was left without a pane of glass intact. But was it really necessary, they asked, for the B.B.C. to broadcast so regularly that there had been "enemy planes over the East Coast"?

Great Yarmouth Town Council considered on February 6th whether they should book an orchestra and make other of the usual arrangements for their summer season, but felt they had to postpone a decision. Two days later another drifting mine blew a gap in the pier at Clacton, damaged the lifeboat house and a nearby hotel and broke most of the sea-front windows. Still the various local councils tried to put a brave face on the situation. Lowestoft previewed a colour film it had sponsored to promote its charms. The Cromer Protection Commissioners decided to reopen in time for Easter the pier which had been closed since the outbreak of war. Hunstanton rather cheekily began to promote itself as a "West Coast resort".

Damage to Clacton pier caused by a drifting mine.   *East Anglian Daily Times*

Easter came, and there was no great rush to the coast. There were few private cars on the roads now, and the railway company did not advertise its customary half-day excursions. About 750 visitors turned up in Great Yarmouth, however, and looked at one or two bombed vessels which were moored there. Lowestoft, Cromer and Sheringham attracted a couple of hundred visitors each. Bunty Carr noted the situation further west:

> "Local holiday camp has twenty guests in — munition workers from Coventry — but *no* bookings for the season. During their stay the Coventry visitors were looking for eggs and onions; they were very short there . . . Visited Hunstanton. At 7.15 p.m. there was one car leaving the car park and two other people in the amusement park. The cinema was the only place that looked alive."

By April, however, decisions about the summer season had to be made. So Great Yarmouth, to take one example, agreed to book an eight-piece orchestra for a season from July 1st to August 31st and made arrangements to open its marina, boating lakes, bowling greens and tennis courts. But even as it did so, events were shaping up for a very different future. Hotel and boarding-house proprietors were closing up large portions of their premises, which they then sought to have re-rated as warehouse accommodation, and retreating into a few rooms for personal use. Nearly a thousand properties in the town were completely deserted. The loss of rate revenue to the council was

32   The Ipswich Gilbert and Sullivan Amateur Operatic Society presentation of *The Mikado* at the Felixstowe Summer Theatre.   *East Anglian Daily Times* ▶

catastrophic and, when it made its new rate in March, it was increased by 3s. 1d. to 18s. 9d. in the pound. Even so, the council had an overdraft of £52,000.

Not all the resorts were in such poor shape, but they all had problems. They had several times been in conference together to debate what they should do and the general hope was that the government would come forward with special grants to tide them over. But there was no encouraging sign of this to date, and now it was resolved to put together a detailed statistical case for presentation to Whitehall officials.

While the resorts wondered whether there would be "a season", people at large wondered if there would be a war—a real, fighting war—and, if so, when and how it would begin. The American press had now begun to write of "the phoney war" and Winston Churchill, later on, referred to this period as the "sinister trance". [8]

It was not possible to find many reliable clues in the behaviour of the nation's leaders at Westminster. The Labour Opposition in Parliament, while it had immediately declared its commitment to the armed struggle against Hitler and Fascism once war had been declared, had no direct responsibility for its conduct. This encouraged a continuing debate in the Labour Party ranks. When Harold Laski, one of the best-known members of the Party's National Executive, attended a conference of East Anglian Labour organisations in Norwich during January he delivered a strong defence of the leadership's war policy. But the conference immediately afterwards passed a resolution, by 44 votes to 16, deploring the "fight to a finish" attitude and proposing an immediate conference of European nations and the United

States "to arrive at a basis for a just and lasting peace". This caused a good deal of controversy, within as well as outside the Party; the Southwest Norfolk Labour Party met at Swaffham and publicly criticised the manner in which a resolution in such terms had been passed.

Sometimes, however, the attitude of the Conservative government seemed almost as ambivalent. Ministers were suspected of thinking that the war could be won, relatively painlessly, by economic blockade of Germany. Chamberlain himself referred to this as "the main weapon" in March, and a couple of months later the Chiefs of Staff prepared a paper which postulated that "Germany's economic difficulties would cause crisis and collapse by the end of 1941. The British Army, therefore, would not have to face battles on the scale of those in the first world war". [9]

It was not unnatural, after the long months during which the German bombers did not arrive and the armies on the western front did not engage, that there was considerable public speculation that the war might soon be over. Some people professed to *know*. A commercial traveller visiting Ipswich confided: "I've a friend who works for a broker in the City of London and he tells me that on the Stock Exchange they are laying odds of six to one that it will all be settled before September."

Market stalls still to be found on Halstead's wide main street. *East Anglian Daily Times*

CHAPTER THREE

On Active Service

OUT IN the North Sea the skies were a uniform grey and bitter east winds kept the water running at storm force. It had been snowing, off and on, for weeks. Spray froze as it fell on ships' rails and tackle, and there were icicles in places. The crew of the East Dudgeon lightship, most of them men from Great Yarmouth, Gorleston and Lowestoft, had never endured worse weather. Soon after breakfast-time on January 29th they heard the roar of an aircraft engine and out of the clouds swooped a twin-engined Heinkel bomber. The men on deck had scarcely spotted the black-and-white crosses on the side of the plane which spelt danger when the first burst of machine-gun fire sprayed the length of the vessel.

The lightship was a sitting target. It could not manoeuvre in order to try to evade the attack, and it had no armament with which to defend itself. The crew took what shelter they could, and waited. Several times the German plane dived on them, its guns blazing. Then it steadied its course above the vessel and released nine bombs. One of them made a direct hit.

No-one knew just what happened after that. In such crises men behave like automatons. Like automatons, they did not even register the icy cold as, somehow or other, they clambered into a small boat and pulled away from the stricken lightship. But then there was the long pull to the shore, an appalling nightmare of misery. For hours they battled against the sea; the cold entered their bones and the energy ebbed from their muscles. Yet they made it to the shore, a deserted beach which, as they surveyed it, was their hope and their despair. The seas were pounding heavily upon it. The spray was almost crystallised ice. And there was no easy way to bring the boat ashore. They left it to the waves to carry them forward and then they jumped. John Sanders, a Great Yarmouth man, waded wildly on to the beach and fell down exhausted. The next wave numbed him and tried to clutch him back, and with a final desperate effort he crawled away from it. As soon as he could summon his strength, he raised his head and looked round for his companions; but he had none now. Of the eight men who had rowed to shore, seven had been too weak to survive the surf. The Sheringham lifeboat went to look for them, but their bodies were washed up on the Lincolnshire shore.

Pilots of the R.A.F. "Kipper Patrol" which watched over the North Sea fishing fleet taken on a good-will trip aboard the old Wells lifeboat *Royal Silver Jubilee*   *R.N.L.I.*

The German Luftwaffe had been attacking shipping off the East Coast regularly since the first days of the war — it was no "phoney war" here. These shipping lanes were dense with merchantmen; on any average day there were well over 300 vessels of one sort or another either at sea or in east coast ports. They usually sailed in convoy — after the end of January this became obligatory in the sealane between the Thames estuary and Cromer Knoll, which was the most dangerous stretch — but even in convoy they could receive only limited protection.

The Royal Navy laid down an immense north to south minefield behind which it was hoped that the convoys could sail without serious interference from enemy surface craft. At the same time the Germans, using planes, submarines and surface craft, spread *their* mines across the shipping channels. The British minesweeping fleet, which included large numbers of commandeered fishing trawlers, went out daily from Great Yarmouth, Lowestoft, Brightlingsea and Harwich to try to keep the channels clear. When they had done their work, however, the swept channels were so narrow that vessels were compelled to steam in double — or even single — line. This meant that a convoy of sixty ships might well be strung out along twenty miles of channel. [1]

An East Coast convoy comprising 24 merchant-men, mostly colliers, with life-boats outswung for instant use.

Eastern Daily Press

They were vulnerable to attack. As 1940 began, none of the merchant ships were armed. They tried to protect themselves with some strange devices: wires attached to rockets which they fired across the path of aircraft, kites and balloons, even harmless fireworks which it was desperately hoped might distract the enemy. Of course, the Royal Navy was always at hand. The sailors had almost completely taken over the east coast ports. Harwich had become a principal naval base, part of the Nore Command. The one-time Great Eastern Hotel had been taken over by the Admiralty at the outbreak of war; the cross-Channel train ferries now shuttled ceaselessly back and forth to Calais with tanks and guns mounted on railway wagons, ambulance trains and lorries, and every manner of military stores; Parkstone Quay received and despatched an endless procession of naval craft; and over the whole estuary there floated two dozen bulbous grey barrage balloons with trailing cables to deter low-flying aircraft. At Lowestoft the Royal Naval Patrol Service had its headquarters at the old Sparrow's Nest theatre, known from March 1940 as H.M.S. Europa; the motor torpedo boats of the Light Coastal Forces had their headquarters at the Royal Hotel, now known as H.M.S. Mantis; the shore establishment of the Minesweeping Flotilla was here, too, known as H.M.S. Martello.

The R.A.F. also had a role. From the Coastal Command aerodrome at Bircham Newton, near Docking in Norfolk, two squadrons of Anson planes flew daily to give inshore convoy protection between the Thames estuary and

37

the Wash. R.A.F. Fighter Command also tried to assist, without much success during the early weeks of 1940. They did not send up fighters until they received a call from a convoy, so that they were always late on the scene. Sometimes they failed to locate a convoy at all; even worse, there were a number of cases when they swooped in so suddenly and so low that the convoys thought they were the enemy. [2] From the end of February it was arranged that fighter patrols would be maintained over the four convoys that were usually at sea at any one time, and a fifth over the fishing fleet on the Dogger Bank, which had also been attacked.

Despite every effort at defence, January 1940 produced a melancholy catalogue of disasters. On the 8th the Lowestoft motor trawler *Eta* caught a mine in its trawl, which exploded when the trawl was drawn in. The vessel was wrecked, but the crew of six were rescued by a sister ship *Rotha* after spending three hours in a lifeboat. On the following day the London steamer *Upminster* was attacked by two low-flying German planes. The crew raced around the deck and ducked behind the funnel as the machine-guns opened up, but the attackers then dropped bombs which sank the vessel. The captain and two men were killed; the ten other crew were machine-gunned as they rowed away in small boats, but they survived and were picked up. On this same day one of the first attacks on lightships took place. Gorleston lifeboat went out to the aid of *Reculver* and later the vessel was brought into Great Yarmouth.

An Avro Anson of the "Kipper Patrol". These aircraft were already out-dated at the beginning of the war but served in a variety of roles, particularly as trainers.

Mrs M. Martin

On January 11th there was a typical attack on the Lowestoft trawler *Celita* when she was fishing with a number of other trawlers. It was her maiden voyage and a German plane picked her for special attention, presumably because she was obviously brand new. No-one was injured, but skipper Arthur Moore reported a terrifying experience:

"He circled and, coming down only a few yards above our mast, he loosed off at us with a machine-gun. All the crew were grouped on the foredeck gutting the fish we'd just taken out of the net and if the gunner's aim had been more accurate we should have been in a bad spot. As it was, the bullets only went through the funnel or glanced off the rail." [3]

On shore people heard a good many explosions during this day. One was when the 5,123 tons Italian steamer *Traviata* struck a mine, burst into flame amidships, and sank. Cromer lifeboat brought thirty survivors ashore, and hundreds of spectators on the cliffs and promenade watched the drama. While the lifeboat was standing by the sinking *Traviata*, German planes attacked a naval trawler *Holyrood* about a mile away, machine-gunning the decks and then dropping four bombs. Two hit the deck rails and fell into the sea and the other two missed — it was one of those narrow escapes from death which seemed incredible but which soon became commonplace.

Three British cargo ships threatened by a Heinkel bomber were saved by R.A.F. intervention. Three Spitfire fighters arrived on the scene just as the Heinkel was circling about fifty feet above one of the vessels; they dived on it from several thousand feet and it hurriedly dropped its bombs and made off. The Spitfires pursued it for forty miles, there was exchange of fire, and the Heinkel was last seen skimming the sea with its port engine disabled and smoke pouring from a wing.

◀ Motor Gun Boats in Felixstowe Dock, showing the very stark nature of these craft.
F. V. Powell

Trawlermen attended to their nets whilst a
third assembled the Lewis Gun.
B.B.C. Hulton Picture Library

The R.A.F. return the compliment. Aircrew
of the "Kipper Patrol" help Coxswain J. E.
Dumble of the Sheringham lifeboat into an
Anson.   *R.N.L.I.*

There was intense activity again on the 12th. There was another attack on
a lightship, the crew of which, although shaken, were not hurt. A Heinkel
bombed an armed trawler, but without causing harm. But the Newcastle
steamer *Granta* went to the bottom when it hit a mine, though its crew was
saved. There was then a comparative lull for more than a fortnight,
punctuated only by the loss of the Greek steamer *Asteria* and thirteen of its
crew when it struck a mine on the night of the 17th, and an announcement on
the 25th that the Lowestoft steam strawler *Newhaven* had been given up for
lost, with its crew of nine, as it was a week overdue from a fishing trip.

And so to the fierce German onslaught on January 29th, when the East
Dudgeon lightship was murderously attacked and four other ships were sunk
and many damaged. German planes ranged along 400 miles of coast from the
Tay estuary to Kent and bombed and machine-gunned at least a dozen vessels.
When the Latvian steamer *Tautmila* was bombed, seven crew were killed and
fifteen others, with the captain's wife, rowed themselves to a deserted part of
the Norfolk coast. The following day the *Tautmila* drifted ashore at Walcot
and another survivor clambered off, and she was eventually refloated and
brought into Great Yarmouth.

40

On the 30th the *SS Royal Crown* was bombed and set on fire. Fifteen of her crew rowed ashore at Easton Bavents and were taken, utterly exhausted, to Southwold hospital. The vessel drifted on to the beach at Covehithe; four bodies were taken from her, and ten others were recovered from the sea. There was an unexploded bomb somewhere in the ship and it was crucial to extinguish the fire which still blazed, so the Auxiliary Fire Service manned a longshore boat converted for use as a fire-float and battle against the flames for many hours, during which time they were machine-gunned. Private George Storey, of the Royal Berkshire Regiment, who went aboard the ship while it burned, was awarded the O.B.E. Weeks later—on February 24th—the *Royal Crown* was salvaged and repaired.

During the two days January 29th and 30th shipping close in to the harbour at Great Yarmouth came under repeated heavy attack and the German bombers swooped over the town itself. "For the first time," the *Eastern Daily Press* reported, "Yarmouth has been witness of aerial activity of a kind that it has been anxious not to have connected with its name." Listeners to the radio picked up the cry "We are being attacked" and the sound of machine-gun fire. Then three dull explosions shook the town and rattled all its windows. Housewives who ran out of doors saw British fighter planes chasing a big grey bomber out to sea. This was an attack on the *Jersey Queen*, a vessel which had formerly been on the Channel Islands run. Soon afterwards those who were on the seafront spotted another large plane circling over town and sea to the southward. Then a patrol vessel in the roadsteads was seen frantically zig-zagging, the plane swooped, two bombs fell and huge water-spouts rose from the sea. The ship was undamaged, and the bomber circled and made two more attacks, and once seemed to be within a few yards of its funnel. R.A.F. fighters then arrived and there followed a battle of hide-and-seek in the clouds.

Eleven ships were sunk by German aircraft along this coast during the month of January. The Admiralty now prohibited any independent sailing during daylight hours, and it was resolved that merchant vessels must be armed. The Home Fleet was asked to give up some of its machine-guns and to provide naval gunners and these men and weapons were transferred from ship to ship for each voyage through the danger zone. It was a stop-gap until more satisfactory measures could be taken. After the end of February the Army was involved, too, and thus began an organisation which was later known as the Maritime Royal Artillery. [4]

Not until April, when the Germans became preoccupied elsewhere, was there any respite in the North Sea war. On the night of February 9th-10th the enemy lay 157 mines off Cromer Knoll and 110 mines in the Orfordness-Shipwash area, without interference; the new field off Cromer caused the loss of six vessels. The clearance of mines was a slow and dangerous business and it was not until April that trawlers began to be equipped with a new sweeping device to enable them to tackle magnetic mines effectively. By that time there was a new hazard: U-boats were constantly active in the North Sea, usually attacking from the surface in the dark and then escaping unseen. Some sinkings attributed to mines at the time were the results of torpedoes.

On February 3rd a convoy north of Cromer was attacked. On the 4th the Lowestoft trawler *Willa* was machine-gunned on the fishing grounds. On the 9th the Yarmouth coasting steamer *Boston Trader* was bombed and machine-gunned and two of her crew injured. On the 13th an unknown ship was found floating bottom up off the Norfolk coast. On the 20th the Lowestoft trawler *Saxmundham* was repeatedly attacked from mast-top height but, though her funnel, wheelhouse, engine-room casing and decks were pitted with bullets, she carried on fishing for several days afterwards. When Skipper H. Head brought her back to harbour he explained: "We must not let them panic us." On the 22nd two German planes attacked the trawler *Outfall* off the Norfolk coast, but she was one of the vessels which had now been provided with a machine-gun and she fought the planes off. On this same day there was a heavy attack on ships in a convoy sailing just north of the Wash. One of them was the *Gothic*, of King's Lynn, which left port that evening to sail with the convoy to Middlesbrough. Her Master, Captain J. Cooper Nisbet, was a veteran of 70 who had often taken his ship into Barcelona through heavy

As the sun set over the North Sea, the Mine Sweeper steamed back to port.

B.B.C. Hulton Picture Library

The Commander-in-Chief of the Nore, Admiral Sir Reginald Plunket-Ernle-Erle-Drax inspecting men of the anti-submarine trawlers at Great Yarmouth. *B.B.C. Hulton Picture Library*

bombing during the Spanish Civil War. This night, while on the bridge, he was shot through the thigh and his second officer received injuries of which he died, but the *Gothic* sailed on. On the 28th the 4,350 tons *Mirella*, of Genoa, went down in two minutes fourteen miles off the Suffolk coast, after an explosion, and sixteen survivors in two boats reached Aldeburgh, completely exhausted, the following day. At almost the same time the *Marie Rose* was torpedoed and sank off Aldeburgh; ten of the crew lost their lives, nine others were found on the shore at Haven House suffering from exposure, and a further seven were rescued from a small boat off Sizewell.

The story was much the same in March: further attacks on lightships, many more arduous turn-outs by the East Coast lifeboats. The Lowestoft steam trawler *Halifax*, making her first trip since the early days of the war, was lost on the night of March 11th, but her crew of nine were picked up safely. At about the same time the 5,335 tons *Amelia Lauro*, of Naples, was bombed and set on fire a few miles off Great Yarmouth; a lifeboat rescued the crew of 29.

Although the Luftwaffe was so active over the North Sea during the first few months of 1940, its aircraft only slowly and sporadically began to cross the coast. There were some German planes over the Shetlands on January 1st, but the first time they were seen flying over English soil was on January 11th. The first enemy aircraft over East Anglia was reported from Suffolk on January 17th, but no warning sirens were sounded. On the 25th searchlights were active and anti-aircraft shells were seen exploding over the coast, but there was no sign of a plane. On the 30th planes few over Great Yarmouth for the first time and it was reported that a raider had been shot down off the coast. During the morning of February 3rd two German bombers flew over Southwold Pier and disappeared to the northward. But the time of planned attack on inland targets in Britain had not yet come.

R.A.F. activity, however, meant that the skies were rarely clear of planes. There were fifteen active R.A.F. aerodromes in East Anglia at the beginning of 1940, and four others were under construction. The principal fighter bases were at Duxford, just south of Cambridge, and at Debden, near Saffron Walden, and the airfield at Martlesham Heath was regularly used as a forward base. Duxford was long-established: it had been a fighter station, charged with the defence of East Anglia, since 1923. It was the first station to have Spitfires — there were two squadrons of them there in the early months of 1940, and a third squadron was re-equipped with them in March. Debden, which had been completed in 1937 and rapidly extended after the outbreak of war, was now an important sector station guarding the southern part of East Anglia and the approaches to London. Two squadrons of Hurricane fighters were based there and a squadron of Blenheim fighter-bombers. [5] Gradually people came to recognise these planes — particularly schoolboys — as they flew overhead and eye-witness stories began to circulate of some of the battles they fought. Scores of people in one east coast town watched a fierce battle between five British fighters and two German planes on March 7th.

Any planes which came down on British soil at this time, however, were British. On March 27th an R.A.F. bomber missed houses in Princes Street, Ipswich, by only a few feet and then fell in the river Orwell, close to the main power station, where it was partly submerged. The crew of three escaped. A few days later a figher pilot who had been wounded in a dogfight between three Hurricanes and two Heinkels off the coast landed in a field near the Norfolk coast rather than run the risk of not getting back to his base.

R.A.F. Bomber Command had its bases in East Anglia early in 1940 at Marham and Feltwell, in Norfolk, and at Honington, Mildenhall and Stradishall, in Suffolk, all with squadrons of Wellingtons. Mildenhall sent some of its planes to Newmarket Heath when the war began and they flew from there throughout 1940. Crews and ground personnel were accommodated in the racecourse grand-stand. There were other airfields, all with squadrons of Blenheim fighter-bombers, at Wattisham, Wyton, Watton and Upwood. Bomber Command's activities in the early weeks of the year were limited. The emphasis, when bad weather did not prevent flying altogether, was on reconnaissance and training. But this activity was combined with the dropping of propaganda leaflets over Germany and the German-occupied territories of Austria, Czechoslovakia and Poland. These "leaflet raids" had begun during 1939 and news of them was scornfully received in some quarters. A pantomime joke at Christmas concerned a warship that had sent a diver down to deliver a leaflet to a U-boat. At the beginning of March, however, a systematic reconnaissance of estuaries and inland waterways on the continent was commenced and plans were made to lay mines in them. On April 6th the leaflet raids were suspended and all was prepared for concentration on mine-laying; but an unforeseen development put a stop to all that. (6)

Vickers Wellington bombers on Marham, Norfolk, aerodrome preparing for the coming night's operations. *Kinsey*

There were many parts of East Anglia, particularly the garrison towns, where the Army was the service most in evidence. In addition to the Territorial battalions, which had been called to full-time service even before the declaration of war, the conscripts were now arriving at barracks. Most of the 21-year-olds had reported by the beginning of 1940 and thereafter they registered and were called up first at monthly intervals, and then even more frequently. Gibraltar Barracks at Bury St Edmunds was one of the main training centres. Virtually all empty buildings in the town, if they were considered large enough for the men "to live a barrack-room life", were taken over by the Army and nearly a thousand men were accommodated thus. "Practically the whole of Bury St Edmunds played its part in becoming the Greater Gibraltar Barracks," wrote Colonel W. N. Nicholson in his official history of the Suffolk Regiment. [7] A new camp called West Lines was built on the Newmarket Road during 1940 to increase accommodation further.

By January 1940 all the professional soldiers in the East Anglian regiments were serving abroad. Britain had an empire and its army was given a variety of overseas responsibilities. The 2nd battalion of the Suffolk Regiment was now in Razmak, on the North-West Frontier of India, engaged in the destruction of hostile tribal towns. The 1st battalion of the Royal Norfolk Regiment was also in India, but preparing to leave; it returned to England in time to be posted to Wimbledon as part of a Guards brigade allotted during the summer to the defence of the United Kingdom. The 1st battalion of the Essex Regiment had been in Egypt since the outbreak of war, and in January 1940 was moved to the Sudan. The other three professional battalions — the 1st Suffolks, the 2nd Royal Norfolks, and the 2nd Essex — had all been posted to France in the early months of the war as part of the British Expeditionary Force.

Thus it was that the 18th Division, which moved into Norfolk in November 1939, and the 55th Division, which moved into Suffolk and north Essex, were composed of Territorial battalions. Some of them were deployed around the coast: the 4th Royal Norfolks were in Great Yarmouth and the 4th Suffolks in Lowestoft; the 2nd Cambridgeshires moved into a hutted camp on

A Y.M.C.A. travelling car which took light refreshment, books etc. to isolated units in the Eastern Counties.

East Anglian Daily Times

46

the edge of the salt marshes at Stiffkey, on the Norfolk coast, during January. Other battalions were assigned to the defence of aerodromes and other "vulnerable points" throughout the region: detachments of the 1st Cambridgeshires guarded the R.A.F. stations, and the 5th Suffolks mounted guard on a variety of "VPs" in an area embracing Horning, Mundesley, Stalham and Acle. One battalion of Territorials, the 7th Royal Norfolks, was sent to France during January, though it was only half-trained.

The anti-invasion plan which was effective before May 1940 was code-named "Julius Caesar". It was dependent upon Army formations which in general "were inadequately trained and equipped for mobile warfare". [8] There was even a serious shortage of anti-aircraft guns and searchlights. Sometimes morale of the men sagged, as revealed in a diary entry by Thea Tregall on February 5th:

> "Heard from Charles B (major, Territorials), still at Bury. His men have all had 'flu or German measles and at one time there were only twenty on their feet . . . He is very disconsolate about staying there so long, and says he feels they are not 'pulling their weight', in view of the things that the Navy is having to put up with."

There is no doubt that the rank-and-file soldiers were pretty bored, with too much time on their hands, and very little money in their pockets with which to seek amusement — after deductions many of them were left with only a shilling a day to spend. A great deal of voluntary effort was made to provide them with comforts and to keep them amused. Concerts were arranged in villages and towns, some of them modest productions with amateur talent, some more elaborate. In Norwich on January 30th the Lord Mayor, the Sheriff and various other dignitaries turned out for a concert in St Andrews Hall to which nearly 1,000 servicemen were invited. The municipal military band, the Norwich Male Voice Choir and a long cast of individual artistes provided the entertainment. There was community singing to organ music; one side of the hall sang the songs of the first world war, *Pack up your troubles, Tipperary*, and the rest, in competition with other side singing *Roll out the barrel, We'll hang out our washing on the Siegfried Line*, and other modern favourites. The Salvation Army, the Y.M.C.A., the Women's Voluntary Service and many other similar organisations provided rest rooms and canteens and the people to staff them. All of these efforts were much appreciated. When, for example, a temporary building was erected in the forecourt of Thorpe station at Norwich to cater for servicemen in transit, 8,000 men took advantage of the facilities in the first five weeks and the fifteen camp beds provided were fully occupied every night. Red Cross and St Johns volunteers provided staff to cover from noon to 6 a.m. every day and the building itself and all its furnishings were provided by gifts and subscriptions. Similar efforts were made everywhere.

Mr Justin Brooke of Wickhambrook seen with some of the 70 Land Army Girls he employed.
East Anglian Daily Times

Of the life of those East Anglians who had been posted overseas virtually nothing was known by their families back home — except for the comparatively small numbers who were given leave early in 1940. The first confirmation that some East Anglians were at the western front was provided by an announcement early in the year. On the night of January 3rd-4th a patrol of six men from the Royal Norfolks was sent to reconnoitre German positions around the railway station at Waldwisse, a village in No Man's Land, about 25 miles from Metz. Captain Peter Barclay and Lance Corporal Herbert Arthur Davis, moving ahead of the rest of the patrol, tried to enter a large house, which appeared to be empty, and were met with grenades and rifle fire from within. They replied in kind and escaped. Barclay, who was a well-known Norfolk sportsman whose home was at Cromer, was awarded the Military Cross and Davis the Military Medal — the first decorations for gallantry awarded to the B.E.F.

In February East Anglians serving in the Royal Navy made the headlines, when British warships entered Norwegian territorial waters to intercept a German vessel, *Altmark*, and release 400 British prisoners-of-war locked in below her decks. Four of the men who were rescued came from the eastern counties and were received home as heroes: Ordinary Seaman Leonard Clarke, of Gimingham, Assistant Engineer Frederick Wall, of Ormesby, Third Officer Leslie Frost, of Brightlingsea, and Second Officer William Platten.

For most of the men who had left England early in the war, however, there had been no excitements, no fighting, but considerable discomfort. The Germans had had a plan to invade Flanders before the end of 1939, but the appalling weather conditions caused it to be set aside. Bitter fighting (in every sense) continued in Finland, which the Russians had invaded in December, but temperatures sometimes worse than minus 20 degrees Centigrade combined with snow, rain and mist made the launching of an offensive in the west unthinkable. Around the middle of January there was a brief alarm, with rumours of German troop concentrations on the Dutch and Belgian frontiers, and on January 14th all B.E.F. leave was temporarily suspended.

Five British divisions were in France by the beginning of 1940, a sixth went out in January, two more in February and a further two in March. Reg Dexter went out in January with the Royal Norfolks:

"I was detailed to accompany the Adjutant to France to arrange billets for the regiment. From Cherbourg we ambled through Normandy and on to the Lille area. In accordance with French military law, other ranks were not allowed to be billetted in private homes, so outhouses, barns and similar accommodation had to be requisitioned.

At one place I had to accept, with my driver, an attractive pig-sty and at another place we were offered the local vagrants' ward of a workhouse, with concrete head-rests on the beds and the walls dripping with water. We declined that bed and breakfast and settled for sleeping in our 15-cwt truck in the local market place.

Some of the first decorations of the War were awarded to Captain F. P. Barclay, the M.C., and Lance Corporal H. Davis, the M.M., both of the Royal Norfolk Regiment.   *Eastern Daily Press*

The regiment duly followed us and took up billets in various villages, mainly mining centres in the vicinity of Lille. R.H.Q. had one or two moves and finished up at Crevecoeur le Grand, where we settled for quite a long period. Our Q.M. Store was in a village primary school and we had our sergeants' mess at the local Café de la Union."

The whole of the B.E.F. took up positions in the sector near Lille, along the Franco-Belgian frontier, but brigades were moved by rotation to the northern outposts of the Maginot Line, near Halstroff, so that they could extend their experience in a sector directly facing the enemy. In fact, there was no great danger at this time and when a first list of war casualties appeared in the *Eastern Daily Press* on the last day of January it included only five men of the Royal Norfolk Regiment, four of the Essex Regiment and two of the Suffolk Regiment.

When the B.E.F. took up its prescribed positions it found that the French had dug out an anti-tank ditch with pill-boxes at 1,000 yard intervals, and there was a continuous belt of wire. The first, and urgent, task was to strengthen these inadequate defences and to extend them in depth. A few mechanical excavators and concrete-making machines were produced, but mainly it was a matter of manual labour. For many weeks the men dug trenches, laid roads and strung wire, usually up to their knees in mud and slush. So far as possible, the officers maintained a training routine; the men turned out wearing balaclava helmets, scarves and mittens. It was so cold that bottles of beer froze solid. Football matches were arranged between units and occasionally concert parties came out from England; expeditions were made into Lille. The local population was not always friendly: when the 2nd Essex Regiment moved to Meurchin in mid-February the officers found that the billets selected for them had been locked and barred. There was no coal, although they were in the centre of a mining area, and very few fires. But, despite the considerable discomfort and the unutterable boredom, morale remained good. Even the unenthusiastic French crowds softened as they watched the Drums of the 2nd Essex Beating the Retreat on the town square at Bruay. The atmosphere of the period was skilfully conveyed by Colonel Nicholson in his story of the Suffolk Regiment:

"During daylight, most men—jerkined and muffled—dug, splashed, sand-bagged and revetted. No 1 Platoon at last drained its trenches; No 2 promptly flooded as a result. Spy scares abounded, as did spies. Farmers explained that in France rabbits were game, not vermin; difficult, this, for the Suffolks to live up to. Madame gave a party for the men in her billet, Monsieur pleaded against a change round of billets; No 3 Platoon were his *garçons*. Marianne, aged six, was spoiled. Yes, they hoped to put in a hot water system, but better wait and see if the Bosches came—a frequent and ominous theme, this. Field of fire or no field of fire, the tree must NOT be cut down; the Bosche had cut down too many trees in the last war. Tomorrow's leave train cancelled. Today's mail late. Hot baths at the nearest coalmine—twenty miles in the rain. Gracie Fields, singer, in Lille. But chiefly MUD— and RAIN."

But never mind. Chamberlain had said that Hitler missed the bus. To reinforce the point, General Sir Edmund Ironside, the Chief of the Imperial General Staff, declared on April 5th: "We have now actually turned the corner."

General Claudel Georges, Commander-in-Chief of Allied Forces in North Eastern France in 1940, inspecting a Guard of Honour from the 2nd Battalion Royal Norfolk Regiment at Marchiennes.
Imperial War Museum

51

CHAPTER FOUR

The Road to Dunkirk

WITH LONGER days and rising temperatures, life in East Anglia was deceptively normal. The cattle, sheep and lambs were turned out on the Norfolk marshes for the season. Neighbours competed to see who could set the most vegetables: weekends were spent planting lettuces and cabbages, putting in potatoes, and sowing peas and beans, onions and turnips. More people licensed their cars and put them on the road again. The Colchester Repertory Company rounded off the best season it had every known, with audiences totalling 72,000. Norwich City Football Club started regular training sessions for youngsters, hoping to recruit new talent to the team. Owners of craft on the Broads made a co-operative arrangement under which holiday-makers would get enough petrol to cruise 25 miles a day. An editorial note in the *Eastern Daily Press* was euphoric:

> "Spring is the more pleasant after a hard winter. In the heart of Norwich the Castle Mound is studded with gold; in the gardens aubretia and purple primrose invite the first butterfly and the still drowsy bumblebee, and the woods ring with the notes of many birds . . ."

If one scratched the surface, however, this cheerful picture dissolved. There was a bright and a sombre side to every situation. The repertory players were going off to entertain troops at home and abroad. The football clubs had only kept going by the most desperate contrivances:

> "The borrowing of players which has been a feature of wartime football reached farcical proportions in the final of the Southern League Cup between Chelmsford City and Worcester City . . . The Worcester side included six Brentford first team men, two from Crystal Palace and one from West Bromwich Albion." [1]

In the field of social services there were a few gains to set against the setbacks. Norwich Education Committee approved a new scheme for secondary education, to take effect from the following September, which was designed to improve the chances of many more children. There was to be a larger entry from primary to secondary schools at the age of eleven and a second review of children's abilities and natural bent at the age of thirteen, when each child would either continue at secondary school or switch to practical studies.

Children at North Walsham Central School enjoying their dinners. 130 were served daily for a charge of 3d per head. *Eastern Daily Press*

Most hospitals were now escaping from the serious financial problems which had limited their pre-war activity. The government had distributed large quantities of instruments, apparatus, furniture, drugs and dressings. Taking the Norfolk and Norwich Hospital as an example, government grants reduced its deficiency from £5,077 in 1938-9 to £2,175 in 1939-40. At Bury St. Edmunds a Ministry of Health grant enabled work to be resumed on a big pre-war extension scheme, which provided 300 extra beds. But the hospitals were, in fact, being paid by the government to keep beds empty, available for air raid or battle casualties. It was now more difficult for the civilian sick to be admitted. [2]

Around the coast, the Spring sunshine encouraged optimism among traders that they might have a summer season after all. Jenny Carr recorded in her diary during April that the local holiday camp proprietor was receiving some bookings for August; but at the same time her sister Bunty noted down some of the new problems:

"Talked to beach cafe proprietress. She had a job to get any stock to start for Whitsun. She said: 'Told me I'd got to write down every single meal I serve. 'Taint likely I shall have time for that. We shall have to have a licence to breathe soon.' "

53

The bigger seaside resorts were getting increasingly anxious about their financial problems. The big increase in the rate at Great Yarmouth had raised a howl of protest. A public meeting was called at Gorleston and 150 ratepayers voted to petition the King to have the administration of the borough taken out of the hands of the town council and given to a government commission. But no-one could say that the councillors were not trying. The Mayor posted a personal letter to 30,000 people in many parts of England assuring them that there was no truth in stories that the town was surrounded by barbed wire entanglements and its population spending most of their time in shelters. The Council also voted for Sunday opening of cinemas — there were seven of them in the town — and for extended shopping hours, to 9 p.m. five days a week and to 9.30 p.m. on Saturdays.

A Budget introduced in Parliament by Sir John Simon on April 23rd increased the postage rate for letters from 1½d to 2½d, raised taxes on cigarettes, beer and whisky (up to 16s. a bottle), and added sixpence to the rate of income tax, to bring it up to 7s. 6d. in the pound. It was not popular. Mass Observation obtained the reaction of one Suffolk villager:

> "I haven't smoked for some time. It's awful, the increased prices. Everything's gone up. About 30 per cent, they say. It's not fair, though, putting so much on tobacco. It's the only little pleasure a lot of people get." [3]

An announcement by the Ministry of Food reminding the public that Meat Rationing was about to start.

East Anglian Daily Times

There was much worse to come, for a supplementary budget later in the year pushed income tax up to 8s. 6d., increased further the taxes on alcohol and tobacco, and raised the levels of surtax and estate duties. There were two innovations in these budgets. The Chancellor of the Exchequer announced "an unusual proposal I have in mind, a new form of tax which, when put into effect, should be the source of a substantial additional revenue in time to come. I propose to call it a Purchase Tax. It is a form of sales tax . . ." Labour M.Ps condemned it immediately as an injustice to the poor and some Conservative M.Ps were convinced it was unworkable. When it was introduced, it was at the rate of 24 per cent on luxury goods and 12 per cent on other purchases. The other innovation was described as "Pay as you go—a new method of collection"; for the first time, tax was to be deducted compulsorily at source from all wages and salaries.

As Rex Porter walked home to his lodgings for lunch on April 9th he noticed that "the pavement was blocked and a police sergeant was trying to move people on". They were around the entrance to a radio shop and the 1 p.m. news bulletin could be heard from within. As he made his way through the centre of Chelmsford he noted crowds of forty to fifty people outside each of the radio dealers, and small groups of people sharing copies of the evening newspaper. The news which caused such excitement was of the German invasion, early that morning, of Denmark and Norway. Now the war had really begun.

Rifle practice for the boys of The Royal Hospital School, Holbrook.
East Anglian Daily Times

It was not easy, in the days that followed, to assess how events were shaping, despite the press and radio coverage. The fact was (although hardly anyone in Britain had any inkling of it) that Britain had been planning an invasion of Norway. The purpose would have been to carry relief to the Finnish Army fighting the Russians and, incidentally, to disrupt the flow of iron ore from Swedish mines, through Norway, to German industry. When the Germans began to occupy Norway, therefore, Britain was able almost immediately to despatch forces to try to dislodge them. A few headlines will indicate how this clash of arms was reported:

Eastern Daily Press	Cambridge Daily News
April 10th	
BRITISH AND FRENCH WARSHIPS IN NORTH SEA ACTION	SMASHING BLOW TO THE NAZI NAVY
German cruiser sunk: steamer torpedoed	Four cruisers reported sunk
April 11th	
BERGEN AND TRONDHEIM REPORTED RETAKEN	NAZI ADVANCE FROM NARVIK STOPPED
Allied navies smash through to mouth of Kattegat	
April 15th	
HITLER'S BLACK WEEKEND	BRITISH TROOPS IN NORWAY
Narvik freed—7 German destroyers sunk	— Official
	Landings at several points

There was, of course, an official censorship and the papers were printing all that was permitted, but the reassuring picture presented left the public badly unprepared for the news when Norway surrendered to the Germans on May 1st. Denmark had been occupied bloodlessly by the Germans in two or three days. The British public was becoming vaguely uneasy before the truth came out; they had noticed increased signs of military activity. Thea Tregall noted in her diary:

"Searchlights tonight extraordinary—they seem to have moved in, so that they all collect around the garden. The beams are broader in the slight mist, and circle the house. There is a plane, but they haven't picked it up."

Once it was known that the Germans had had a major victory, reaction took various forms. Bunty Carr's diary notes:

"Mother ordered two tins of sardines off both tradesmen calling today, because she thought we should not get any more from Norway."

Another Mass Observation diarist, in Cambridgeshire, noted:

"First thought is we shall get no more Danish butter and eggs, and paper will be scarcer."

Some of the troops back from Norway lining the decks of a transport
East Anglian Daily Times

She was right. The *Cambridge Daily News* transformed itself from a broadsheet to a tabloid newspaper, and the *Eastern Daily Press* was reduced from ten to eight pages each morning. At the same time, it made a bold innovation: news replaced advertisements on the front page.

People now began to feel that there had been a dramatic deterioration in the war situation. The Carr sisters in Norfolk noted the new anxiety. After hearing of the German success in Norway, Jenny made this diary entry:

"It worries me as to what he (Hitler) will do next. He seems to get nearer. Bunty thought of packing a bag—also Jimmy, but he can't see why it would be any safer the other side of England. Mr W. came in. He says he thinks they will pack their 'go-kart'—he would have to take that to put the dog on."

On the same day Bunty Carr reported:

"Went to see a neighbour who is Spring-cleaning. She had a very old mac. on the line which she said she was airing in case she had to flee. She thought if you were a refugee you wanted to look as scruffy as possible, and then they would get up a fund for you."

The mood of M.Ps at Westminster was quite different. Most of them felt angry. A debate in the Commons on May 7th was made the occasion of a fierce attack on the way the Chamberlain government was conducting the war. The dramatic climax came when Mr Leopold Amery, a respected elder statesman of the Conservative Party and a long-time friend of Neville Chamberlain, turned to the Prime Minister and, quoting the words with which Cromwell had once addressed the Long Parliament, cried: "You have sat too long here for any good you have been doing. Depart, I say, and let us have done with you. In the name of God, go!" In the vote which followed, the government's customary majority of well over 200 was cut to 81. The direct outcome was the resignation of Chamberlain and the formation of an all-Party Coalition government headed by Winston Churchill.

A Mass Observation representative, reporting from the Suffolk village of Hollesley, quoted a typical reaction:

"A man in the Hollesley main street, looking at a newspaper and talking to friends: 'Now we've got a real government, old boy.' " [4]

On the day that Chamberlain resigned Germany invaded Holland, Belgium and Luxembourg. By the time the new Churchill government faced Parliament for the first time on May 13th this new campaign, to which Germany had committed 89 divisions, was virtually decided. Dutch resistance collapsed after five days' fighting and the Belgians capitulated on May 27th-28th. Winston Churchill promised the Commons and the country "nothing but blood, toil, tears and sweat".

The new Prime Minister, Mr Winston Churchill.

Eastern Daily Press

Once the Germans were established in Norway and Denmark, R.A.F. Bomber Command began regularly to raid targets between Stavanger and Aalborg, and the bases at Feltwell and Honington participated in these operations. The Luftwaffe continued to fly against England. There was one particularly daring episode during the night of April 22nd, when enemy seaplanes alighted on the sea not more than two miles off Felixstowe, presumably to lay mines. Shore guns opened up on them.

The following week, on Tuesday, April 30th, the German air force for the first time carried death and destruction to a town in England, and the town was Clacton. A Heinkel bomber which was mine-laying off Harwich was spotted just before midnight when it broke out of seamist and cloud. A.A. guns opened fire on it and shells damaged its tail and destroyed its rudder. The plane flew on: over Clacton, where it circled twice, then out to sea, then back towards Holland-on-Sea. As it crossed the coast again it lost height. It came low over a recreation ground, as though trying to land, but it struck a house and tore its way through several others. The mines it was carrying exploded. Two civilians were killed and 162 injured, thirty-four of them sufficiently seriously to be detained in hospital. Fifty houses were wrecked and every building within half a mile had its windows blown out and its ceiling brought down. Among the buildings shattered was a nursing home which had a number of maternity cases at the time. There were still four hundred evacuee schoolchildren from Edmonton in Clacton at this time, but none of them was hurt. The A.R.P. services, in this first major test of their efficiency, "acquitted themselves with credit". [5] The four members of the crew of the aircraft were buried in Clacton with full military honours, their coffins covered with many flowers.

59

Officials inspecting scattered fragments of the bomber at Clacton-on-Sea after a German aircraft carrying a cargo of mines was shot down.   *B.B.C. Hulton Picture Library*

It is interesting to note how wildly inaccurate rumours spread after an incident such as this. A young shop assistant in Chelmsford described in his diary how his manager went out, on the morning after the crash, to buy a newspaper, failed to get one, but . . .

"Comes back, says he's been talking to a man who's seen a paper and he says the plane came down near Clacton station. It was full of mines and damaged two rows of houses and 100 actually killed, according to him. In the afternoon, Mrs S and her daughter both tells me it was mostly children who were hurt. My aunt tells me that someone told her it was a little place outside Clacton where the plane came down. My sister says she thinks the German plane crashed in Clacton on purpose. They knew they'd got to come down, so thought they'd do a little damage. Could have landed in the sea." [6]

According to a report which appeared in the *Essex County Standard*, however, an eye-witness declared: "The plane was on fire. Several Verey lights were thrown out of it, and the pilot was apparently trying to find some place to land."

60

At the end of April all shipping movements between Harwich and the Continent were suspended, but early in May two vessels, *Malines* and *St Denis*, were sent to Rotterdam to bring home British subjects living in the Netherlands. They were in port there when, on May 10th, German forces invaded Holland and bombed Rotterdam. The *St Denis* was scuttled and abandoned, and Captain Mallory, with 178 passengers on board the *Malines*, found his way down the unlighted river to the sea and came back safely to Tilbury. Not long afterwards the British destroyer *HMS Hereward* brought Queen Wilhelmina and her suite from the Hook to Harwich. Other destroyers brought the Crown Princess* and her family and Dutch ministers and diplomats to England. The Dutch gold reserves and stocks of diamonds were brought across on May 11th and a cruiser, *Jacob van Heemskerck*, with an escort of one destroyer and seven submarines of the Royal Netherlands Navy took refuge in Harwich. [7]

By the time of these events the British troops in northern France had completed very extensive additional defences along the frontier with Belgium. They had constructed 400 new pill-boxes and dug forty miles of revetted anti-tank ditches. Many new airfields had been created, new roads and railways laid, and large base installations completed. [8] But they were very inadequately armed. There was no armoured division in the B.E.F. and the three divisions which had most recently arrived had no artillery and were short of even ordinary unit weapons and equipment. [9] But the time had come for them to fight, and the battle was not to be on their carefully-prepared front.

The sudden German attack, or at least the speed of its advance, was a surprise. Men of the Essex Regiment were awakened on the morning of May 10th by the explosion of bombs falling only a few miles away and continuous heavy A.A. fire. "This was the first indication of anything unusual." [10] They learned of its significance by tuning to a B.B.C. news bulletin. Reg Dexter, with the Norfolk Regiment on another sector of the front, recalls:

> "I'd been to Lille to a concert at which Gracie Fields appeared, and we'd only just got back to our billets a little after midnight when there was a mighty thumping of bombs in the direction from which we'd just come. From then on we seemed to be constantly on the move . . ."

Within 48 hours most of the B.E.F. had moved forward into Belgium, including the 1st Suffolks, the 2nd Royal Norfolks and the 2nd Essex. They took up a line from Wavre to Louvain, north to south, about fifteen miles east of Brussels. The most graphic account of those days has been provided by Colonel Nicholson in his history of the Suffolk Regiment. Orders came through on Sunday afternoon, May 12th, to move to Louvain. They travelled most of the night, stopping to bivouac at 4 a.m. By this time crowds of Belgian refugees—and some Belgian troops—were streaming back in the opposite

*later Queen Juliana

61

direction. The message was clear: the Germans must be advancing swiftly. During the day that followed they tried to keep themselves concealed, but they watched German planes swooping down to machine-gun the columns of refugees. At nightfall the Suffolks moved forward again, now keeping to side roads in the pitch black night. Conditions were difficult. The head of the column turned up a sunken lane and some of the transport bogged down in mud; it took an hour to get everyone back on the right road again.

As dawn broke on May 14th the battalion came into a wood called Eiken Bosch. In the first pale light they saw that it was carpeted with lilies of the valley. Away in the distance they could see the spire of Louvain cathedral. But there was something strange about the countryside before them, which it took some moments to comprehend. There were no people and no vehicles in that landscape and the animals were displaced from normal context — they were roaming freely amid the wheat and barley. Presently, planes flew overhead and shelling began, quite close at hand, and by then the men of Suffolk were energetically digging trenches, putting up barbed wire and positioning such anti-tank guns as they possessed.

On this same day German forces advanced on to French soil. A powerful thrust through Luxembourg and the Ardennes by-passed the much-vaunted Maginot Line of French fortifications. German motorised columns penetrated the French lines and moved rapidly towards the French Channel coast, away to the south of the British forces. Within six days they were to reach Abbeville, sealing off British, French and Belgian forces in a northern pocket.

But the regiments of the B.E.F. knew little of this, as yet. The Royal Norfolks were in action on the 15th. They were repeatedly dive-bombed, though their casualties were light. One company shot down a dive-bomber with Bren guns. But they were worried about the vagueness of the information trickling through about the German advance. The 2nd Essex battalion found themselves on the 14th without orders and unable to move. Two days later they moved into Brussels, where they began blowing up bridges to delay the German columns.

On May 16th the B.E.F. received orders to withdraw westward, in three stages, to the river Scheldt. The Suffolks began their withdrawal at 1 a.m. on the 17th, just three days after they had dug themselves in before Louvain.

> "The battalion retired through Brussels, pausing in some public gardens on the west side of the city. It was a hot sunny day; the streets were full of civilians and it was plain they could not understand why the Army was moving in a westerly direction. But they were very generous with their gifts of all kinds, from biscuits and cigarettes to bottles of wine. Except that some streets were covered with broken shop window glass, where neighbouring bridges had been demolished, there was no suggestion that the enemy would be into the town that night." [11]

By 2 a.m. on May 18th the Suffolks were back on the river Dendre, and by 7 p.m. on the following day they had reached the Scheldt, where a stand was to be made. They dug themselves in over an area contained within a curve of the river and they tried to make themselves comfortable:

> "While holding this line on the river Scheldt, a battalion 'farming' organisation was working well; where possible, one man was detailed to milk the cows, whose udders, owing to their being in 'full milk', were soon streaming, another to collect the eggs, another to water and feed the cattle and poultry. The battalion butcher was employed to kill a pig, steer or calf; this variety in messing was much appreciated." [12]

But the battalion came under heavy fire and suffered many casualties, including its Commanding Officer, Lieut. Colonel Fraser, who died on his way back to England. The difficulties were compounded when, at 3 a.m. on the 20th, the Suffolks were ordered to break off from their river-bank engagement, move to Watrelos on the Belgian-French frontier, and launch an attack southward against the Germans who were now building up their strength towards the Channel. This attack met with heavy opposition and resulted in a withdrawal, with 75 casualties.

In London, the Cabinet was by this time "examining a possible withdrawal towards Dunkirk if that were forced upon them". [13] On the 20th arrangements were in hand at Dover for a large-scale evacuation, and on the 23rd all British forces still facing eastward were withdrawn to the defences they had constructed during the winter along the French frontier, from which they had advanced only twelve days earlier. On the same day the B.E.F. was placed on half rations.

The Royal Norfolks, meanwhile, had been in the thick of some of the fiercest fighting, in the course of which the first of this regiment's five Victoria Crosses in World War II was won. It went to Company Sergeant Major George Gristock, 22 years a soldier. Just after dawn on May 21st closely-packed masses of German infantry launched a furious attack and outflanked part of the Royal Norfolks' position. Gristock collected eight riflemen and led them forward to cover the exposed flank. Alone, he crawled forward to try to silence a machine-gun post, was hit and severely wounded in both legs, but went on to within 20 yards of the enemy and then opened fire. With four shots he killed the German crew of four. He made his way back and continued to direct the defence until the line was restored. The official citation stated: "By his gallant action the position of the Company was secured, and many casualties prevented." But George Gristock did not live to be presented with his decoration.

There were horrors ahead without redeeming honour. The fierce fighting continued until the 25th, by which time the Royal Norfolks were holding a front of about 5,000 yards with barely two full-strength companies.

"About 90 officers and men were eventually forced to surrender. They were marched to a paddock in the village of Le Paradis, hastened on their way with kicks and rifle butts. There they were mown down in cold blood by two machine-guns. Two men, Privates Pooley and O'Callaghan, survived. Badly wounded, they crawled from under a heap of corpses and were tended by a French farmer and his wife, until they were recaptured by Germans and removed to hospital." * [14]

The British plan was to withdraw to a bridgehead covering Dunkirk. For the Suffolks, May 26th saw the beginning of the final retreat. Advance parties left for the coast and the battalion proper jettisoned much of its equipment and began to retire to the Yser. Soon two of the platoons had been overrun by the pursuing Germans, who were also developing a dangerous flanking movement. On the 29th, when the position was critical, the Suffolks withdrew further, through heavy shellfire, and at 7 p.m. on the 31st they were told to make for the beach at La Panne.

The men of the 2nd Essex Regiment were already on the beaches at Dunkirk on May 29th, and the Royal Norfolks arrived there on the 31st. Reg Dexter remembers the last few days like this:

*Privates Pooley and O'Callaghan survived to give evidence at a War Crimes Court and the German officer responsible was hanged.

"As we progressed slowly towards Dunkirk we were amazed at the destruction en route. Dykes and canals were filled with abandoned wrecked lorries and fields each side of the roads were strewn with equipment, dead horses of the French and Belgian cavalry, miles and miles of the flotsam of war. We reached La Panne, and along the beaches we were harassed by shelling off-shore, shelling from the land at our rear, bombing and machine-gunning from the air.

On the last day of May we arrived at the outskirts of burning Dunkirk and made our way to the beaches. There were rows and rows of men there, waiting to be taken off. I sat on the sand and ate my last bit of rations—a tin of peaches. A man near me had a wireless set he had taken from one of the derelict houses, and Jack Payne's Orchestra was playing from London."

A member of the staff of the *Eastern Daily Press* who was also serving with the Royal Norfolks sent a descriptive report to his paper. In one village:

"It was the same scene as everywhere else—houses mere burnt-out shells, and worse; bodies here and there. In one doorway lay the body of a woman. By the corpse sat a baby crying—the only living being, apart from the military column moving through. Then, a few yards ahead of me, a soldier—an English soldier—stopped and snatched up this pitiful infant. He carried it with him, and that baby he brought back to England with him." [15]

The Suffolks moved cautiously into La Panne on June 1st, for the streets were full of abandoned vehicles, some burning fiercely, and ammunition lorries exploding. The place was being systematically shelled. Thousands of men were waiting on the sand-dunes. At dawn German planes appeared and machine-gunned the beach and the water's-edge. Thousands of rifles were raised and discharged against them. Later came dive-bombers. Until 4 a.m. on this day troops were being embarked from La Panne, but those who arrived later found they had to face a gruelling march southward along the beaches to Dunkirk. They took it at a slow pace, with a ten minute halt every hour. When they reached Dunkirk, the beach was being shelled and in the town, where fires were blazing, there seemed few walls still standing and no roads without craters.

In the end, 225,000 British officers and men, as well as 110,000 French and 2,000 Belgian troops, were evacuated from these beaches. For them, it was a miraculous delivery; but there were many who did not come back. When the remnants of the 2nd Norfolk Battalion was assembled in England, there were but five officers and 134 men, of nearly one thousand who had been sent to France eight months earlier. The battalion had all but been destroyed.

The evacuation involved an amazing feat of organisation in Britain. From May 20th naval officers made a complete survey of all suitable ships in harbours from Harwich round to Weymouth, and searched all boatyards from Teddington to Brightlingsea. Three of the bigger ships which had operated out of Harwich took part in the evacuation: *Malines* (2,969 tons), *Prague* (4,218 tons), and *Amsterdam* (5,092 tons). After making three round trips to Dunkirk, the *Prague* was holed by a German bomb on June 1st. With one engine out of action, Captain Baxter beached her near Deal, the 3,000 Frenchmen on board were transferred ashore, and later she was salvaged. Four Harwich paddle steamers were also in the rescue fleet. *Waverley* embarked 600 men in the first day of the evacuation and began the return passage when several Heinkels swooped and bombed her; she sank quickly, with 400 soldiers still aboard. The other three, *Marmion, Duchess of Fife* and *Oriole*, carried on for four days and nights without sleep and brought nearly 5,000 men to Dover.[16]

There were unexpected and unfortunate problems when the Royal National Lifeboat Institution was asked on May 30th to send as many of its vessels as possible to Dover to assist. First of the boats to leave their stations were the *Abdy Beauclerk* and the *Lucy Lavers*, both from Aldeburgh. Great Yarmouth, Gorleston, Lowestoft, Southwold and Walton also sent their boats. By the time they reached Dover, however, a problem had arisen between some of the Kent lifeboats' crews and the naval authorities. A correspondent writing in the *East Anglian Daily Times*, who said he had been allowed to see the R.N.L.I's official report, gave this account of events:

> "On receiving their orders these crews (of the Kent boats) raised questions as to their feasibility, also as to the conditions of service, and ultimately got rather to loggerheads with the naval people. This, unfortunately, culminated in their refusing duty and being sent home. Thereupon the authorities arranged for naval ratings to man the lifeboats on arrival, and the other crews were given no option but were sent home by train, while naval parties took over . . ." [17]

There were other East Anglian sailors whose desire to take part was thwarted. Crab and whelk boats from the North Norfolk harbours made their way to Dover when a phone call to Sheringham suggested that more volunteers would be welcome. Men tossed a coin for the chance to join the crews. When a hint came that some of the Blakeney crews might be incomplete, Sheringham volunteers waited on the beach until 3 a.m. and were bitterly disappointed when they saw the Blakeney boats sailing past without stopping. Fifteen or sixteen boats reached Dover, and some were away for eleven days, but in the end they were not allowed to cross the Channel – only boats capable of 15 knots were used. But they did valuable patrol work and landed troops from trawlers.

Bolton-Paul Defiants which had initial successes when introduced over the Dunkirk beaches.

A naval officer sent to Lowestoft to seek vessels rang his superior to report that he had secured eight boats, but had crews for only six. While he held on, his superior rang an East Coast yacht club and explained the position. "It was 8.45 p.m. and there were a few yachtsmen chatting over their drinks. Back came the answer: 'We're on the way'. When they reached Lowestoft they set off immediately for Dunkirk." [18]

Not until the exhausted, blood-stained warriors arrived at Dover and were packed into troop trains which fanned out across half of southern England was there a general appreciation of their sufferings. Then Red Cross and W.V.S. workers were on the platforms distributing tea and cigarettes, food and chocolate, and they could read in men's faces the ordeal they had endured.

May 27th was a National Day of Prayer, and when the Dunkirk deliverance was fully understood many churchmen claimed a divine intervention had kept the Channel waters calm. There was certainly a quite exceptional volume of prayer; congregations were some of the largest ever seen in East Anglia — 1,500 in Norwich Cathedral, Bury St Edmunds cathedral packed to the doors, chairs in the aisles for some of the 1,400 congregation in St Michael's at Beccles, over a thousand people in many churches all over the region. As they walked to church that morning, people at several points along the coast, as far north as Felixstowe, heard the continuous, distant rumbling of gunfire drifting across the water from Belgium and France.

CHAPTER FIVE

A Change of Mood

IT HAS sometimes been claimed that war is a great leveller: that everyone is "in it together". It may be true that everyone shares suffering, but the glory and the hardship is no more evenly spread that are the privileges and the poverty in peacetime society. The extent to which normal activities continued in East Anglia while the men of the county regiments went through Hell on the other side of the Channel is quite astonishing.

On May 30th, when the last British defence in Belgium was collapsing and most of the troops were on or near the beaches, a series of open-air concerts began on Christ's Pieces in Cambridge — "a well-dressed and lively song and dance show called *War Time Tonics*." A comedian presented himself as a German parachutist, making his exit on a scooter. On Saturday, June 1st the greyhound stadiums at Boundary Park, Norwich, and at Great Yarmouth drew their usual crowds; Cambridge Town was beaten by Walthamstow Avenue 6 − 2 in the final of the East Anglian Cup; at Beccles, seven boats raced for the Coronation Cup; the Royal Norwich Golf Club played their June medal match. On Sunday, June 2nd the pianist Solomon gave a recital of Haydn, Debussy and Brahms music in the Cambridge Arts Theatre. Monday, June 3rd — Dunkirk was in ruins and the evacuation was nearing its end — brought an announcement that the Derby and the Oaks would be run at Newmarket ten days later. The week of Dunkirk, for the gardeners, began with the potatoes coming through; it ended, according to a Bury St Edmunds diarist, with "irises and lupins out in the garden".

At Cambridge some undergraduates were trying too hard to maintain business as usual. The Union Society announced a debate on the motion: "That this House welcomes the imminent overthrow of Western Civilisation". Immediately, the Proctors intervened, they interviewed the Chairman of Debates and, according to a statement issued on May 27th, the Management Committee of the Union reluctantly decided "without dictation or intimidation from the University Authorities" to discontinue all debates until further notice. [1]

There were over 6,500 undergraduates at Cambridge at this time, only a few hundred fewer than a year earlier. Six evacuated London colleges were quartered there: the London School of Economics at Peterhouse, Bedford College for Women at Newnham, Queen Mary College at Kings and Girton,

Pont l'Eveque, watched by Service personnel, leading the field in the 1940 Derby run at Newmarket.
B.B.C. Hulton Picture Library

the School of Oriental and African Studies at Christ's, St Bartholomew's Medical College at Queens, and the London Hospital Medical College at St Catherine's.

A Traditional May Week programme was arranged, though with fewer events—the usual college balls were abandoned. But the Madrigal Society proposed to sing again beneath Kings College Bridge, the bumping races were arranged, the Footlights announced a special performance in aid of the Red Cross, and the Labour Club planned a "Midsummer Carnival" at the Dorothy Cafe. On May 31st, two days before this programme was due to begin, the Vice Chancellor convened a meeting of Heads of Houses, the Heads then reported to the governing bodies of their colleges, and that same evening undergraduates who had completed their examinations were instructed to leave Cambridge without delay. Some colleges turned them out within 24 hours.

On the other side of the region, at Great Yarmouth well over a thousand delegates booked in at hotels and boarding houses for the Women's Co-operative Guild Congress, attended a civic reception and chatted with the Mayor, and then settled down to several days of earnest political debate. Traditionally, this organisation had a near-pacifist attitude, but on this occasion it was muted.

The realisation that Britain was in peril came slowly to the public. A Mass Observation representative reported from the Woodbridge area during the battle in Flanders:

"A man at the modernised Cherry Tree pub in Woodbridge observed: 'They're not telling us enough. We can't tell what's going on, except that there's a terrible battle, with men being mown down like corn, almost. I don't like the look of it at all."

A woman in Shingle Street: 'My, they are getting close now. I reckon they'll be over here before long. They're just waiting their chance." [2]

On May 31st Bunty Carr wrote in her diary:

"Next rumour started: that invasion is expected tonight, and all to be ready. Played tennis with schoolmaster until 9.30 p.m. S. said: 'This reminds me of Drake'. Mother said: 'No one but you would think of playing silly games.'"

People who lived near the coast were now genuinely apprehensive, but they discussed the possibilities in a spirit of bravado. The Mass Observation representative heard an A.R.P. warden call out to a bus driver:

"Let me know if you see any of them para fellers about, Harry. I don't want them to be disturbing my pullets now they've just come to lay."

Airmen practicing the use of respirators whilst marching through Cambridge.

Cambridge Evening News

Jenny Carr's diary contains this remarkable entry:

"This morning we were lying in bed and Mother called out: 'What's that noise?' I listened and heard machine-gun fire. It was louder and nearer than any I have heard before. We laid in bed and listened and heard burst after burst of guns. This was about eight o'clock. Mother called out: 'Do you think they're landing on the beach?' She then said: 'If they come, I shall get under the bed and lay low.' Bunty said: 'I think I shall be more of a success with them if I stay in bed.' We all laughed, and after a time it stopped and I went to sleep again."

An increase in tension had been generally noticeable, nonetheless, after April 9th, when the German forces moved against Norway and Denmark. The tension deepened with the occupation of Holland in May. Enemy forces were now in position only sixty miles from the coast of East Anglia. According to one well-informed commentator, there had been a "complete failure to take the possibility of invasion into account at any time before the middle of May, 1940". [3] After May 10th innumerable orders were issued and new procedures put into operation. All Service leave was stopped. Orders were issued: "Respirators to be carried at all times." Among civilians, more carried their gas-masks with them, but there was still a majority which did not.

The night the German forces reached the Dutch coast and stood facing Britain, soldiers were posted at ten-yard intervals along much of the east coast, on duty for two hours at a time and then being relieved. Rex Porter, who by this time had been called up and was stationed at the Seacroft Camp at Caister, provided Mass Observation with a detailed narrative of events throughout that first day and night:

"In the afternoon one of the Pioneer Corps old soldiers drew my attention to one of the Lewis gun posts in this camp. 'Look at them three b-----s standing by that gun. Any other afternoon you'd have a job to get anyone to stay there; now they all want to be there to have a go at Jerry if he comes over.'

At the end of tea, the orderly officer came in and gave us instructions as to how we were to clear out of the camp in the event of a night air raid. He added: 'It doesn't matter if you forget your trousers, so long as you have your respirator, which brought a big laugh.' "

Porter then listened, with about sixty others, to the 6 p.m. B.B.C. news bulletin. There was a general "Ssh" as it began, to produce absolute silence. When a low-flying aeroplane was heard, very close at hand, there were apprehensive glances to the window, but no one moved and the silence was unbroken. The news that seventy German planes had been shot down brought a "Coo" of satisfaction.

"The advice at the end of the news about challenges by sentries caused a bit of amusement, because the Non-Combatant Corps has just started doing guard here, and the sentries are armed only with sticks. The prospect of us coping with a German parachutist armed with sub-machine guns struck us as funny . . .

Around 10 p.m. our section sergeant called us all together and gave another of his solemn warnings. He made what he had to say sound as if if had come straight from British Secret Service agents in Germany to our company office. 'You lads know what we're up against tonight. They're expecting a raid any time. What they're expecting is parachutists. They'll be armed, you know, and you aren't. There'll be only one thing for you to do — run like Hell. (Titters) I'm not joking. It's deadly serious. If we get a raid, you've got to scatter and if they try to make a landing, then you've got to scatter further still.' "

While all this was going on, searchlights were very active to the southward and an atmosphere of expectancy soon produced a rumour in the camp: "They're off Yarmouth". Rex Porter's narrative continues:

"I had been feeling a little funky. I was shivering a little and was chewing gum with abnormal waste, spitting a piece out and putting a new piece in every five minutes. But I soon recovered, saying: 'I rather wish something *would* happen.' Here we are, eight months of war and I haven't yet heard anti-aircraft gunfire.

At about 10.30 p.m. a pail of hot cocoa came from the cookhouse and was doled out. As the period of waiting grew longer, an atmosphere of rather forced cheeriness and facetiousness began to develop and we laughed at the most ridiculous things. About 11 the R.S.M. came round to our section sergeant and conferred with him for a while."

In fact, the night passed without incident, until . . .

"At 4.50 a.m. we were suddenly roused by shouts of "stand to". But nothing happened. Later heard that a German plane had been seen by beach guards about 4.45, but it had been chased out to sea by Spitfires."

At the other end of the county Bunty Carr noted how the people in her village were behaving. Those who had put cars into storage were getting them out, filling them with petrol and starting them up, in case they should be needed at a moment's notice. People were putting things together, so that they would be ready to move out. An old pensioner told her that he had £40 in silver coins, which he had been collecting for such an emergency. The two young Carr sisters, living alone with their widowed mother, wondered what they should do.

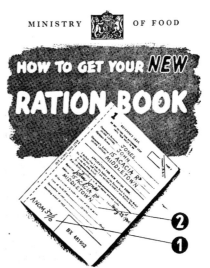

MINISTRY OF FOOD

HOW TO GET YOUR NEW RATION BOOK

Inside the back cover of your present Ration Book you will find a detachable postcard headed 'Reference Leaf' (shown above). Fill in the required particulars carefully. Cut out the whole postcard, address it to your home Food Office (see Note 3 below), and post it, without a stamp, *as early as possible* before Saturday, June 1st.

1 You must write your *National Registration* Identity Number at the bottom left-hand corner of the postcard. Copy the letters and figures very carefully from your Identity Card.

2 When filling in the postcard, remember: Give the street number of your house. If you are on holiday give your *home* address. If you are moving your home before June 24th give your *new* address. Hospitals and Boarding Schools are regarded as home addresses.

3 On the other side of the postcard write the name of your *home* Food Office. (If you are moving before June 24th, or have moved since last September, you must write the name of your *new* Food Office.) Ask the Post Office if in doubt.

Your new Ration Book will be posted by June 24th to the address you have given. When it comes, write your name and address AT ONCE on the pages of coupons and on the counterfoils for rationed foods. This will prevent delay in the shops during Registration. The period for the new Registration with retailers is June 24th to July 6th and not before.

CUT OUT THIS ADVERTISEMENT TO HELP YOU

The decisive struggle has begun in earnest. Our fighting forces are at grips with the enemy — at grips with all the armed power, the brutality and treachery that Hitler can bring to bear. **No one among us can feel safe again until this fight has been won.**

Calm courage and inflexible determination to win this war will be our answer to the challenge. But what can we stay-at-homes **do**?

The answer is plain. We must throw the whole of our resources into the fight **now**.

Get this clear — every National Savings Certificate and Defence Bond you take up is a blow at Hitler and his foul plans for the conquest and enslavement of us all. Every War Savings Group is a fortress firing volley after volley against the enemy. The Post Office Savings Bank and the Trustee Savings Banks are defence lines that we ordinary folk, men, women and children can garrison with our savings.

Now is the testing time. Surely, the least we can do is to back up the men who are risking their lives to defend us. Turn out your pockets and purses. Go without everything that can be given up or postponed. Your savings are needed **now**. Put all you can into National Savings **today**.

The fight being brought home to the civilian population by means of Government advertisements. *Eastern Daily Press*

73

"Everybody round here has it in their minds about what we shall do if invaded. Most people seem to expect it. Most have very wild ideas about what we ought to do. Why have we not had instructions? Since the war not a word to the civil population on what to do on enemy invasion. I wonder if the government has any plans? Everyone here is wondering if we stay put or hop it, if they land. We keep debating the subject of fleeing or remaining, and do not know whether to pack a case or not. We had had our handbags ready, with banknotes in, since the day war was declared."

The smaller worries of life now passed almost unnoticed: the shortage of green vegetables after the severe weather earlier in the year, the reduction of the sugar ration from twelve to eight ounces, the poor quality of the meat, the announcement that there would be only four ounces of butter per person per week after June 3rd—a halving of the ration.

Evacuation of school-children was considered essential, but the occupation of Belgium and Holland by the Germans "immediately made completely useless a large part of the carefully-drawn plans and timetables". [4] The possibility of invasion was now accepted, the danger-map of Britain had changed, and some of the railway lines which it had been intended to use for evacuation of schools were now virtually monopolised by military traffic. All children living within ten miles of the east coast, and they still included a large number who had been evacuated from London earlier in the war, were now warned to prepare to move inland. Designation of the new evacuation areas, and the actual transfer, took place in stages. On May 16th it was announced that children from the Essex coast would be taken to South Wales on May 19th. On May 26th it was announced that children would be evacuated from the stretch of coast northward to Great Yarmouth, and they left on June 2nd. On May 28th the evacuation zone was extended as far as Cromer.

Most of the children were taken to South Wales, the border counties and the Midlands, and the movement was not completed until July. It was not a compulsory evacuation, but heavy persuasion was used. All state schools in the coastal belt were closed, and most of them remained so for the remainder of 1940. The authorities were disappointed to find later that large numbers of children had stayed at home; Great Yarmouth and Lowestoft each had 3,000 remaining. They constituted something of a social problem though there was widespread reluctance to recognise the facts openly. Even before this time Lowestoft Education Committee had set up a committee of enquiry to consider the well-being of young people in the town, which had increasingly taken on the appearance of a naval base. Great indignation was expressed that such a committee of enquiry should even be considered, and its report was received with hostility in some quarters and was, in practice, ignored. The significance of the affair must be read between the lines of this press account of the committee's report:

"The matter was not raised because of any trouble which had arisen, Lowestoft standards comparing very favourably with those of the country as a whole, but because it was felt that in unsettled wartime conditions additional guidance and help might be of assistance . . .

The committee unanimously suggested that the Education Committee be asked to consider the advisability of making representation in the proper quarter for the appointment of women police for the duration of the war . . .

The advisory committee also made a suggestion that instruction in schools should, at the discretion of head teachers, be given to boys and girls on the simple facts of life, but on consideration the Education Committee decided not to issue any instructions on this matter." [5]

At the outbreak of war there had been many thousands of aliens settled in Britain, many of whom were Jews who had escaped from persecution under fascism and who were passionate anti-Nazis. They were rounded up and examined; about 500 of them were interned, 6,800 were placed in a so-called B. Category, which meant that no-one was certain about their "absolute reliability", and the remainder were issued with certificates of reliability. From time to time, there were demands for tougher action against them. The Member of Parliament for Sudbury, Colonel H. W. Burton, suggested in the Commons in March that enemy aliens living on the east coast might have signalled to German planes, thus helping to sink British ships. He called for all aliens to be removed from the area.

After the fall of Holland, the British government put aside all inhibitions on this subject. In Cambridge, as one of the Fellows noted:

"The racket began on May 12th, when my Sunday lunch was disturbed with the tidings that the police had arrested three of my pupils. They had, in fact, arrested and interned all male enemy aliens under sixty . . . The wives of some of the senior men were left without support and had to be provided for locally. A certain number of University lecturers were also removed, and there was a shortage of examiners in law . . ." [6]

On that and the following day, Cambridge police in plain clothes called at the residences of a large number of male enemy aliens and took them by car to the Guildhall. They were later taken by bus to internment camp. Elsewhere in the region, similar action was being taken. Sixteen Germans and Austrians were arrested in Norwich, and a further eighteen elsewhere in Norfolk. By the 16th all Category B male aliens had been taken into custody, and soon afterwards all women in this category, with their children. They were removed to the Isle of Man. At the time, public opinion was in support of this policy, but government and public quickly revised their views as news of the treatment of the aliens trickled out. Then followed remorse, accentuated in July when many aliens who were being shipped to Canada in the *Arandora Star* lost their lives when the vessel was torpedoed. The War Cabinet soon afterwards agreed to release all aliens who were known to be actively hostile to the German and Italian regimes and, at the same time, responsibility for the internment camps was transferred from the War Office to the Home Office.

In May and June, however, xenophobia was unrestrained. On May 22nd Parliament passed an Emergency Powers (Defence) Act, which authorised the government to issue Defence Regulations covering every aspect of life. One of the first, known as Regulation 18B, led to the arrest and internment of Sir Oswald Mosley and eight of his lieutenants, a right-wing M.P. called Captain A. H. Ramsay, and many other British subjects about whose reliability there were doubts. Activists of the British Union organisation, generally regarded as fascist sympathisers, were arrested in considerable numbers, including three in King's Lynn, two in a nearby village, two in Lowestoft and two in Eye. What became known as the Treachery Bill prescribed the death penalty for anyone found guilty of assisting enemy forces or impeding British operations. The imprecation "Fifth Columnist"—a term first used in Spain during the Civil War to indicate a traitor within the gates—was freely thrown about. It did not help when the Commander in Chief of Home Forces commented:

> "My experience is that the gentlemen who are the best behaved and the most sleek are those who are doing the mischief. We cannot be too sure of anybody."

At Woodbridge it was rumoured that the vicar of a nearby village had been arrested — "they say he got up in the pulpit and said Germany was right and we were wrong." [7] In Colchester it was related that a spy had been caught using a radio transmitter. Bunty Carr reported a new rumour almost every day:

May 21st: "J. has talked to a man who tells him there's a Fifth Columnist in the village, who is being watched day and night."

May 24th: "Today village is full of spy stores and rumour of Fascist arrests."

May 25th: "Rumours of several Fascists locked up, including one in next village who had a transmitting station in his cellar."

Before long, there were suggestions that the Carr sisters themselves were suspect. All strangers and non-conformists were eyed warily. Newly recruited commercial travellers, replacing men who had been called up, had to proceed with caution. A Mass Observation representative who visited East Suffolk soon after a plane had crashed there reported:

"The atmosphere at the Butley Oyster pub was tense with suspicion . . . At Eyke there were groups of women talking in the street and they turned and stared suspiciously at me. The atmosphere was so difficult, almost hostile, that I left. Obviously it was hopeless to get into conversation with anyone in village streets." [8]

Many in high authority were as gullible as the ordinary man in the street. When General Ironside first became C-in-C Home Forces on May 27th he noted in his diary: "Fifth Column reports coming in from everywhere . . . I have put piquets on all over the place tonight. Perhaps we shall catch some swine."* [9] Little more than a month later, much wiser, he added his postscript on the Fifth Column: "One is persuaded that it hardly exists." Dr R. V. Jones, F.R.S., who was a member of British Scientific Intelligence at this time, relates in his book *Most Secret War* that he was sent to investigate a spy scare in Norfolk. The evidence appeared to be overwhelming. An R.A.F. officer commanding an airfield near the Wash reported that German planes were changing direction overhead, and that a nearby radar station was troubled with jamming. The electrical engineer in a small town nearby was the obvious suspect, particularly when it was found that he had appeared on the same platform as Sir Oswald Mosley. The local police had had handed in to them a six-inch local map which had been found near a public footpath, which had been marked with what appeared to be bearings on the radar station. It was found to belong to the electrical contractor's brother.

If ever there was a cut-and-dried case, this seemed to be it. Dr Jones was the only one who showed some scepticism. The houses of the two men were raided: a theatrical performance, with soldiers surrounding them to provide

* The Lord Ironside.

Women Observers from the Suffolk village of Benhall who watched the skies for enemy parachutists.   *East Anglian Daily Times*

covering fire, as the local Chief Constable and Army commander dashed up the garden paths and hammered on the front doors. In the electrical contractor's house they found a small box, carefully hidden away.

"It was locked; we asked the engineer for the key. He astonished us by saying that he had never seen it in his life. This appeared to be an obvious lie. The policemen fiddled with the lock and ultimately got it open. They gave a yelp, and handed it to me in triumph. There, inside, was an induction coil, some wire, and some crocodile clips . . . There were some instructions inside the lid. I read them and realised that this was an electrical hair-remover. His wife, modest woman, had bought it for her personal use and had been practising a mild deception on her husband."

General Sir Edmund Ironside (later Field Marshal Lord Ironside) who was appointed Commander in Chief of Home Forces in May. *Imperial War Museum*

One by one, all the damning clues were similarly demolished and perfectly rational explanations were found for every circumstance. When he revealed the story Dr Jones commented: "As far as I could see at the time, and still more in retrospect, the Fifth Column in Britain was completely imaginary." [10]

People of Britain must learn this

IF YOU KNOW...

... exactly where a bomb fell

... what time it fell

... what the bomb just missed

... how many aeroplanes there were

... what they were trying to hit

... which direction they came from

... which district they were over

...KEEP IT TO YOURSELF

and make others do the same

No matter how many other people know things too, no matter how true it all may be, before you talk remember this—IF IT'S TRUE the enemy can use it, IF IT'S NOT TRUE the enemy is using you

JOIN BRITAIN'S
Silent Column

the great body of sensible men and women who have pledged themselves not to talk rumour and gossip and to stop others doing it

THIS ANNOUNCEMENT IS ISSUED BY THE MINISTRY OF INFORMATION IN THE INTERESTS OF NATIONAL SAFETY

Government exhortation to the public.

"UP HOUSEWIVES AND AT 'EM!"
says Herbert Morrison

HOUSEWIVES OF BRITAIN! You have a great part to play for victory. The country urgently needs your waste paper, bones and metal.* They help to make vital war supplies. You are striking a blow for your homes and your children when you save every bit of paper, bone and metal and put it out carefully. Go into action today!

*Also put out waste food if this is collected in your district.

Paper, cardboard, cartons, make cartridge wads, rifle and shell cases, food containers for the troops.

Bones make glue for aeroplanes, explosives, fertilisers to help crops, feeding stuffs.

Metal makes aeroplanes, tanks, guns ships.

Put out your PAPER METAL BONES

PUT THEM OUT CAREFULLY Follow the instructions you will receive. Care saves time, space, money.

THEY WILL BE COLLECTED Councils in districts with a population over 10,000 must arrange for collection. You can help to see that the collection is well and thoroughly done. Send suggestions to your Council.

THEY WILL BE USED Every scrap that is put out according to instructions is efficiently collected will be used for victory.

This is what your back door should look like on collection day.

METAL   BONES   PAPER

ISSUED BY THE MINISTRY OF SUPPLY

East Anglian Daily Times

For a time, however, even an unguarded expression of opinion about the conduct of the war could be dangerous. Alfred Duff Cooper, who was just settling in as a new Minister of Information, urged that all British patriots should regard themselves as members of "The Silent Column"—vigilantes determined to prevent the spread of defeatist talk. Critics dubbed them "Cooper's Snoopers", but their evidence secured the conviction of numerous people who had spoken carelessly or foolishly. A 30-year-old woman telephonist employed at Colchester Post Office got into conversation with three soldiers, while walking her dog on Clacton promenade and, discussing political matters, remarked that "German rule would not be so bad". She was sentenced to three months imprisonment, but it was reduced to a fine of £20 on appeal. At Mildenhall two brothers found themselves in court after a conversation with two soldiers, and were fined £5 each for "publishing a statement on matters connected with the war likely to cause despondency". A clerk in Bury St Edmunds, rushing during an air raid to the ambulance station where he was a voluntary driver, shouted to people who came to their doors when the sirens wailed: "Get in quick, there's a gas attack". That, at any rate, was the evidence against him, and he was fined £3 for action likely to cause alarm — but his version was that he shouted a warning that there was a raid near the local gasworks. Most convictions of this kind which were taken to appeal were quashed, common sense asserted itself, and on July 22nd Winston Churchill told the Commons that the Silent Column had "passed into innocuous desuetude".

There were, however, other clear and specific offences for which offenders were punished. One was the taking of photographs of defence subjects. During May and June several men were fined, at Norwich, Felixstowe and Cromer, and their films and cameras were confiscated. Early in June a Mundesley man was arrested by the Army and brought before a special sitting of the magistrates at Cromer, charged with possessing "a diary, in his own hand-writing, recording measures for the defence of certain places". After two adjourned hearings and a statement that the case had been referred to the Home Secretary, nothing more was reported about it. It was not unusual for courts to be cleared during the hearing of such cases.

There was one minority group whose views, although they were un-popular, were tolerated to a remarkable degree: the pacifists and con-scientious objectors. In the first world war they had been very harshly treated in prison or when taken forcibly to Army units. This time Parliament had decreed clear rules for their treatment even before the war had commenced. There were not many of them, but Cambridge and Norwich produced a much higher average than the country as a whole during the early months of 1940. When the 25-year-olds registered on April 6th, there were thirty conscientious objectors among the 1,000 conscripts in Norwich — about three per cent, and this was matched at Cambridge when the 27-year-olds registered on May 25th, and twenty-six out of 744 declared themselves objectors. Later, the numbers were much reduced. They were all required to appear before a tribunal to state their case why they should be excused full military service, and to indicate what form of service they were prepared to accept. The tribunal at Cambridge, which heard all East Anglian cases, consisted of a county court judge, a professor and a trade union representative. When it met on May 6th one applicant was an itinerant evangelist from King's Lynn, who said he had preached in every county in England in the previous four years and whose only desire and ambition was to win souls. He was registered unconditionally, which meant he could carry on as before. Another applicant was a Yarmouth bricklayer's labourer, who declared that his father had returned from the first world war to live in poverty, that his mother had died in a mental institution, and that his own experience led him to have nothing to do with war. His name was removed from the register, which meant that he was called up for service. In most cases, the Tribunal's decisions fell between these two extremes; particular forms of non-combatant service were specified, such as the Royal Army Medical Corps, or applicants were directed to work in agriculture or, in some cases, were told to remain in the jobs they held, if these had social value. By the summer of 1940, the West Suffolk War Agricultural Executive Committee was employing about eighty conscientious objectors.

They were, of course, widely reviled. The retiring Bishop of St Edmundsbury, the Right Reverend Walter Whittingham, in his farewell message, included the comment: "What a travesty of true Christianity the statement and position of the pacifists is, or so it seems to me." The Mayor of Lowestoft, Major S. W. Humphery, remarked: "I loathe a C.O. I say that such a thing does not exist." He urged that no public authority should employ them, and that policy was adopted by most of them. The Isle of Ely Education Committee decided in May to sack all elementary teachers who registered as conscientious objectors and recommended managers of non-provided schools and governors of grammar schools to do the same. Norwich City Council took a softer line; it voted that all C.O's on its staff should be granted leave of absence without pay for the duration of the war. Ipswich Town Council resolved in July that it would not dismiss objectors.

Men of the 6th Battalion of the Royal Norfolk Regiment place "dragon's teeth" steel girders into position at a road barrier at Sheringham. *Imperial War Museum*

Those who went into the non-combatant units of the Army seem to have fared well enough. Rex Porter was one of them. After his first few weeks in a camp under N.C.O's of the Auxiliary Military Pioneer Corps, all veterans of the first world war, he reported to Mass Observation:

"From the beginning there's been not the slightest demonstration of hooliganism towards any of us from the other side. 'You've got your views,' an old sweat will say, 'and I've got mine', and he leaves it at that. Our N.C.O's have been decent and matey . . ."

In May the bombs began falling on Britain, the first few in Kent on May 10th. The next fell at Felixstowe and Orford on May 22nd; there was a great deal of noise, but little damage. The first casualty in East Anglia is believed to have been a soldier on duty at a searchlight site at Strumpshaw, near Norwich, whose foot was blown off by a bomb during the early morning of Sunday, June 2nd.

The time had come when the Regional Commissioner was to exercise his considerable powers. A defence regulation passed on May 31st provided the authority for him to control and direct all operations of the civil defence services in East Anglia. The Regional War Room at Cambridge now became the battle headquarters: intelligence centre and the centre of operational control. A.R.P. controllers throughout the region fed through to Cambridge information about all incidents due to enemy activity and the steps taken to deal with them. Twelve-hour situation reports were compiled at Cambridge and transmitted by teleprinter to the Home Security War Room in Whitehall, indicating the number of bombs dropped, their location, and the damage caused. [11] But none of this removed from the local authorities their responsibility for the local control and efficiency of the services.

The Army, on its own authority, imposed restrictions. Even before Dunkirk, soldiers were stopping traffic at road blocks all over the region and checking identities:

"All cars were stopped by sentries in steel helmets and with fixed bayonets and drivers made to show their identity cards. Between Mersea and Tolleshunt D'Arcy there were as many as five road blocks." [12]

On May 31st orders were given for all signposts to be taken down, all milestones uprooted and all names of streets, railway stations and villages to be obliterated. There were no half measures. An historic milestone which had been erected in 1729 by Trinity Hall, bearing the arms of the college and the inscription "1 mile to Great Saint Maries Church Cambridge", had the word "Cambridge" chiselled out of it—to the great annoyance of some university men.

Sign posts, with names familiar to East-Anglians, removed from their positions to confuse the enemy.   *Kinsey*

The sale and possession of maps and guide books was banned in some areas; retailers near the coast were instructed to remove their stocks of such material inland. Camping was banned anywhere within ten miles of the coast. It was decided, too, that church bells should be rung only as a warning that parachutists or airborne infantry were descending. (13)

Events had transformed the mood of the people — or most of them. Some there were still whose spirit was lightly brushed by the perils of war. Bunty Carr came upon some of them:

"Went down to beach in evening and found only two evacuee mother friends singing by the breakwaters and the three children in the middle of about twelve sand castles. They said: 'We don't pay no attention to the news now. We've got so as we don't care. We sit out here all day. My husband said first we would be here for five years, then he said ten, and later twelve; but yesterday he wrote and said two months. That's why we're so happy.'"

And another Mass Observation correspondent reported that, a fortnight after the Dunkirk evacuation had been completed, the end of a drought had supplanted the war as the main subject of conversation in rural Suffolk. "Nice drop of rain we've had," they said. "That'll do some good."

CHAPTER SIX

Preparing for Battle

WHEN THE Dunkirk evacuation had been completed, Winston Churchill faced Parliament. "We shall defend our island, whatever the cost may be," he told them. "We shall fight on the beaches, we shall fight on the landing-grounds, we shall fight in the fields and in the streets, we shall fight in the hills. We shall never surrender."

What he did not tell them was that Britain did not possess the arms and equipment with which to put up an effective fight if an invasion had taken place at that time. The situation was indeed desperate. The defence chiefs were convinced that, if the Germans attacked, they would try to land on the gently shelving beaches of East Anglia, behind which there was relatively flat country over which their tanks could advance towards London and the industrial Midlands. The Army's Eastern Command, which was responsible for the south-eastern part of England as well as East Anglia, had only six infantry divisions available. Every one of them had less than half the normal establishment of 15,500 men. They all had less than half the appropriate number of field guns, there was only a handful of anti-tank guns between them, and a serious deficiency of machine guns. As for transport:

> "The bulk of the troops, if ordered to move faster than they could march, would do so in hired motor coaches driven by civilians unprepared for the conditions which might await them in the event of a German landing. Arrangements had been made to assemble these vehicles and their drivers at 'short notice'; but 'short notice' meant that at least eight hours, and in some instances a whole day and night, would elapse before the troops could start." [1]

Conscious of these military inadequacies, the War Office had already, immediately after the German advance into the Low Countries, resolved to raise a force of Local Defence Volunteers.* On May 14th Anthony Eden appealed over the radio to all men between the ages of 17 and 65 who were "capable of free movement" to join up immediately. That same evening they were queuing up outside the police stations all over the country. Among the first of 1,000 volunteers in Chelmsford was the bishop of the diocese, who had been calling for a force of this kind and who now urged on his flock with the declaration: "This is a war against Satan." Within a week, a quarter of a million men were reported to have enrolled in the country as a whole.

---

*On June 26th Winston Churchill sent a memorandum to the War Minister: "I don't think much of the name 'Local Defence Volunteers' . . . I think 'Home Guard' would be better." Within two or three weeks the name was changed accordingly.

Broomsticks did duty as rifles at the parade of volunteers at the Cambridge Town F.C.

Cambridge Evening News

Some men were actually on duty within hours of Mr Eden's broadcast. The Zone Commander at Cambridge called for volunteers to guard the telephone exchange in St Andrews Street and twelve men with borrowed rifles fell in; they were relieved the following day by a platoon of the London Scottish. L.D.Vs from the university mounted guard on the Regional Commissioner's headquarters.

There was, of course, very little equipment for this new force. About one third of the early volunteers were issued with rifles of military pattern. The others had shotguns, sporting rifles or such improvised weapons as heavy sticks and bludgeons. In response to another appeal, a miscellaneous collection of 20,000 firearms arrived in police stations, including several from the gun-room at Sandringham and a number of ancient muskets from Norwich Museum. In Essex, a former naval rating formed a 24-strong Cutlass Platoon. [2] A company commander in Cambridgeshire sent his men out with bags of pepper and lengths of lead cable.

As more arms and ammunition came through, L.D.V. officers loaded them into their own cars and distributed them around. Usually, it was a matter of two or three rifles and a handful of cartridges to each village. An officer who did this in south-west Cambridgeshire afterwards recalled:

"Three hundred and fifty rifles, with ten rounds each, and 350 denim overalls were rushed out and left at Melbourn police station, from where they were collected by the battalion commander and issued through companies to the homes of the village detachment commanders, often without even a chit to say their number, or a signature to show who had them. One remembers a handful of rifles dumped on the billiards table of the village inn, with ducklings waddling in through the door, and the air of subdued excitement and anticipation everywhere one went.

'Any news of the invasion, sir?'

'No'.

'Well, I suppose it will be coming along in due course', and everyone thought it was, and appeared to be utterly unafraid, although we were raising an army as ill-equipped as that of Monmouth at Sedgmoor to face the most highly trained and mechanised troops in the world." [3]

Instructions on what to do "if the INVADER comes", and men of the Stoke-by-Clare Home Guard who would have helped to defend the country in the event of an invasion.

At Ely eight hundred recruits turned up at the Corn Exchange on Sunday, May 19th, and after being formed into sections by parishes marched across to the police station to be kitted.

"Denims were of three sizes: 5, 6 and 10. If your figure didn't correspond, it was just too bad. The caps were all 6¾-in; if you normally wore a 7¼-in, you just had to remember that there was a war on . . .

Observation posts were quickly chosen and manned each night at dusk by nucleus garrisons. It was originally ordained that the whole of the L.D.V. force would muster at alarm posts every time the siren sounded, even if the men lived several miles away from their posts. This order was varied from necessity after there had been three sirens in one night and some men had cycled backwards and forwards eighteen miles between 10 p.m. and dawn . . .

The parades of the trained men were encouraging; they 'jumped to it' in a most inspiring manner. It was better, however, when one merely listened and didn't look as well; the precision of the arms drill and the way they kept step was rather marred by the extraordinary appearance caused through the fit of the denims and, above all, the ridiculous 6¾-in sized caps perched on the top of shining craniums. One avoided, where possible, giving the order 'About turn', because it was perfectly certain that it would result in the temporary loss of at least thirty per cent of the caps." [4]

The L.D.Vs were told that their primary function was to deal with parachute invaders. They were to man observation posts from dusk to dawn, to warn of any hostile paratroop descents, to try to shoot paratroops before they landed and, failing that, to mop them up before they could become organised bodies. Every village had its observation post and soon all roads to towns and villages were barred at night. These road blocks were formed with farm carts, harrows, old cars, scrap iron, willow poles — anything they could lay their hands on. The Volunteers of Cheveley, a village just outside Newmarket, dragged an enormous tree trunk across part of the road and one night, when they were short-handed, they contrived to get the whole squad pinned down by it, helpless until someone came along and then called the A.R.P. wardens to the rescue. [5]

The Army Council issued an instruction: "This is a citizen force organised on the principles of equality of service and status. There is, accordingly, no system of ranks, though there are appointments suitably graded for the commanders of the various formations." Some units took full advantage of the theoretical democracy. The Regional Commissioner on May 15th named Major General Sir Arthur Mills, a retired Indian Army officer, as L.D.V. Organiser in East Anglia and at the same time the Lord Lieutenants of the counties nominated other retired officers as Zone Commanders. These Zone Commanders were expected to choose organisers in each locality, but in some places the L.D.V. elected or acclaimed their own. At Hauxton, a village just south of Cambridge, the 29 Volunteers gathered in the schoolroom and went through a careful voting procedure, with three candidates. Later, this same village group debated the best way of manning its observation post, one faction favouring all-night turns of duty, the other advocating a system of two-hour shifts. A motion was proposed, an amendment was put and carried by 17 votes to 12, and (as the Company Log/Minute Book noted) "Amendment became substantive motion and was carried."

Bunty Carr's diary entries in the second half of May chronicle the adventures of a Norfolk garage hand who rushed to volunteer:

May 15: "J. announced that he is joining anti-parachutist brigade.

May 17: "J. joined last night and says he is going on duty tonight with his neighbour, who was told to go to a very lonely place and said he daren't go there in the dark alone."

May 21: "J. says he shall bring his gun to work every day now. I suggested he keep a bottle of water in his pocket to empty quickly into the petrol tank. It would be better than a lot of shooting and they'd get about two miles away before they found out."

May 25: "J. says they were sworn in for parashooters in his village last night. J. says he is allowed to shoot anybody on the spot now. If we want any of our pets destroyed, we have to pay someone else to do it, and yet he is actually quite prepared to kill a man . . ."

May 27: "J. says he has left the parashooters. They've all left in his village because the major tried to run it like the army."

While the Local Defence Volunteers settled down, the regular Army was constructing additional defence works all over the region. Soon the improvised road barriers which the L.D.V. had erected were being replaced by sandbags or concrete blocks, beside which weapon pits were dug. The Royal Engineers blew gaps in most of the east coast piers during the last few days of May; at Clacton they did it without consulting anyone and caused considerable damage to the lifeboat *Edward Z. Dresden* in her boathouse.

On May 27th General Ironside was appointed Commander in Chief of Home Forces and two days later the Chiefs of Staff gave him their view that invasion was imminent. He began immediately a full-scale reassessment of the problems and the preparation of a new anti-invasion plan. An Invasion Warning Committee met in Whitehall every day from May 31st, sifting whatever evidence there was of German intentions. After studying the tide tables, they came to the conclusion that there was only one week in each lunar

Men of the Royal Scots Fusiliers in training on Frinton beach after their return from France.

Imperial War Museum

month when conditions would be suitable for an invasion attempt. During that week the most vulnerable beaches were at points further northward each day; conditions for a landing in Norfolk were suitable five days later than in Sussex. [6]

As Ironside began his urgent planning, he had three forward divisions in East Anglia: the 18th in Norfolk, above a line drawn inland from Lowestoft; the 55th in Suffolk, above a line extending inland along the river Stour; and the 15th between the Stour and the Thames. Behind them he had an armoured division in Lincolnshire and a corps of three divisions well to the north of London. The new "Ironside Plan" of defence was presented to the Chiefs of Staff on June 25th. The basic concept was that defence must be in depth, embracing the whole of the eastern counties. The Maginot Line psychology which had brought disaster to France had emphasized the inadequacy of so-called "Linear defence". So now the probable invasion beaches would have only a "crust" of entrenched forces, which might harass an invasion fleet and pass back information but which would be unlikely to be able to beat off a determined assault, though they would be expected to stand and fight to the last man. As Churchill saw it, too, "the battle will be won or lost not on the beaches but by the mobile brigades and the main reserve". [7]

The main reserve was to be held ready in the east Midlands, behind a strong barrier of anti-tank obstacles constructed — taking advantage of such natural obstacles as waterways and steep inclines — along a line extending from Bristol to Maidstone, then northward to the Thames at Canvey Island, north-westward through Cambridge to the Wash, and thence to Richmond, in Yorkshire. Between this armoured line and the coast there were to be a series of "stop-lines" and blocks, and a number of small fast-moving units which would deal with parachutists and airborne troops. Five of the forward stop-lines ran across the eastern counties, and there were to be as many blocks and pill-boxes as possible, to be manned by L.D.Vs with rifles. The divisions of the field Army already in East Anglia would remain in front of the G.H.Q. defence line and, taking advantage of the stop-lines, would confine, break up and delay any advance from the coast until the divisions from the reserve had been brought forward. The whole purpose was to "prevent the enemy from running riot and tearing the guts out of the country, as had happened in France and Belgium." [8]

Each port was the subject of a special study, and the cardinal principle was that they should be able to meet an assault from the sea or from landward. Every aerodrome, radar station and fuel depot was to be defended by a special garrison and "vulnerable points" — bridges, power stations, depots and the more important factories — would be under constant armed guard. All large open spaces were to be broken up by obstacles or trenches to impede the landing of airborne troops. Detailed plans were made for the destruction of port facilities, cutting of telephone and telegraph links, immobilising of road transport and railways, and cratering of key roads. [9]

The Ironside Plan was accepted. Much of the defence work it called for was already well in hand. By the middle of June most of the 786 field guns available had been sited near the coast to cover the most likely landing places. A large number of guns had been "borrowed" from the Admiralty, from a pool intended for the arming of merchant vessels, and with these 46 new batteries were added to the coastal defences, each consisting of two 6-inch naval guns and two searchlights. Because the Army was so short of men, the Navy also provided the gun crews for the first few months. [10]

The strengthening of the coastal defences left the GHQ line extremely weak in armour for some weeks, until more was delivered from the munitions factories. Ironside, therefore, moved his armoured division, which had 178 light tanks, southward from Lincolnshire to a position between Northampton and Newmarket. There it was poised to strike either to the east or the southeast, to meet an invasion from any expected direction. [11]

By the third week in June there were tens of thousands of civilians, as well as troops, working on the additional defences in East Anglia. But Churchill, who toured the region at this time, railed against the use of any troops for this work:

"All the labour necessary should be found from civilian sources. I found it extremely difficult to see even a single battalion on parade in East Anglia during my visit." [12]

Many of the civilian contractors, although they made a lot of money, did not satisfy Army standards:

"A large number of road blocks proved useless, as armoured vehicles could go round them; some pillboxes were sited facing the wrong way, or so placed that they could not be occupied by troops or served no useful purpose." [13]

Another problem was discerned by a Mass Observation representative who visited coastal Suffolk:

"There are violent feelings among those *not* employed in government against those who are getting two and three times as much money for labouring and concreting in the area, and who are said often to be people imported from outside." [14]

Decisions concerning stop-lines, and even more so in the case of pill-boxes and blocks, were largely left in the hands of local commanders and there was no time for paper plans to be prepared. In Cambridgeshire:

"sappers prepared bridges for demolition and inserted the charges, and life became more and more hectic. A period of unco-ordinated effort

◀ A heavy gun covering the beach.

ensued. At one time there were elements of five different field companies coming daily to the area. Colonel Clayton (L.D.V. officer) went out one afternoon to inspect progress on a defensive position which was being constructed by sappers and infantry. Five hundred yards away another party was constructing another series of positions; neither party knew anything about the other." [15]

Lieut. Col. Darrell Ovey, D.S.O., inspecting men of the Stowmarket Home Guard.

East Anglian Daily Times

The L.D.V. was now shaking down well and the Prime Minister proposed that the coastal defences should increasingly be entrusted to them. "Bring an even larger proportion of your formed divisions back from the coast into support or reserve, so that their training may proceed in the highest forms of offensive warfare and counter-attack," he urged Ironside. [16]

In the inland areas the Home Guard took over most of the road blocks. They inspected the identity cards of everyone passing after dusk. They stopped all vans and lorries, to make sure there were no German troops hidden away in them. Sometimes a post received instructions to stop a vehicle with a particular registration number; any person or vehicle which did not stop when challenged was fired on. A motor-cyclist who tried to rush a post near Wisbech was brought down by the first shot. Two teenage girls were wounded by shots one evening and had to be treated in hospital at King's Lynn. In other parts of the country, a few people were shot dead. The Home Guard had a very difficult task:

"We were still short of arms and uniforms. There was a certain amount of moral backing in stopping cars at midnight when properly armed and in uniform, but it was not so easy in a mixture of khaki and plain clothes. Late one night an L.D.V. corporal attired in an L.D.V. armlet, civilian overcoat and bowler hat, and armed with a 12-bore gun, held up an officer at a road block. The officer was highly indignant and was refusing to prove his identity.

" 'It's O.K. by me, sir. You can stop here until a real officer comes along — that is, if one turns up before I go to work at 6 a.m. Bill, just take this ------ along and lock him in Payne's cowshed." (17)

In July one million World War One .303 rifles arrived from the United States. Churchill insisted that they should be rushed by special train to the areas where they were needed. One hot summer afternoon ten large lorries rolled into Cambridge, carrying eight thousand of them and they were dumped overnight in the Corn Exchange. When they were examined next morning it was found that they were thickly coated in grease. Within a few hours 150 women volunteers, bringing their own overalls, paraffin and rags, had settled down to clean them. At times their number increased to 250, but still it took a full fortnight to get the rifles ready for issue. As they were distributed, the limited number of .303 rifles which had been handed out earlier were reclaimed for issue to the field force.

The Home Guard was also issued with lethal devices known as "Molotov Cocktails": bottles, of many sorts and sizes, filled with a mixture of petrol, tar oil and paraffin. The thrower had to light a fuse attached to the neck of the bottle and then hurl it at the target. When the glass broke, the explosion might be enough to set a tank on fire: that, at least, was the hope.

"Unfortunately, many of the bottles had leaky corks and there was considerable risk of the thrower's backward movement of the arm setting his uniform on fire. On one occasion a platoon commander had just thrown one of these missiles and was explaining to his men that they were foolproof and that there was nothing to be afraid of.

Whereupon Private Buggins stepped forward from the ranks, halted three paces from the platoon commander, and saluted smartly.

'Yes, Buggins?'

'Excuse me, sir, the arse of your breeches is on fire.' " (18)

The decision to dig trenches on large open spaces caused a crisis at Newmarket, where the famous Gallops were threatened. The Jockey Club was up in arms, and made representations to the local Army chiefs. They were not unsympathetic.

"The officer in charge of the excavator was spoken to on the telephone and it was found that his instrument of destruction was booked for at least a year. The Newmarket Gallops continued to be the training centre for racing, as vital to the nation as any other training centre. Higher authority was placated with tree trunks laid across the Gallops." [19]

Under the cloak of more normal Home Guard activity, there was now created the nucleus of an underground resistance movement which would go into action only after German forces had occupied British territory. With headquarters at a large country house in Berkshire, Major Colin McVean Gubbins brought this highly secret force into existence. He divided the coastal territory of Britain into twelve sectors and in each he appointed an "Intelligence Officer". Each of these men, aided in turn by a "striking force" of a dozen soldiers supplied by Gubbins, was required to form a series of local resistance cells, each with six men. The organisation in East Anglia was made the responsibility of Andrew Croft, son of the vicar of Kelvedon, Essex. He was an intellectual – on the staff of the Fitzwilliam Museum at Cambridge – and man of action – an Arctic explorer and leader of a military mission to the hard-pressed Finnish Army.

In June 1940 Croft made his headquarters in a barn at the rear of his father's vicarage and concentrated on forming units in Essex and that part of Suffolk around Woodbridge; that was the area, he felt, that invaders might seek to occupy first. Later the headquarters was moved to Framlingham and units were formed throughout East Anglia. Croft picked well-to-do farmers and fruit growers, many of them officers in the first world war, to lead most of his resistance groups. Each was allowed to nominate his own men, who were then screened by Croft. There was never any formal enrolment, nor were records kept. Underground hideouts were constructed, usually deeply hidden in woods. They were dug out at night and the earth was immediately carted away from the sites. When completed, they were large enough to accommodate six men and they were equipped with bunks, cooking stoves, Tilley lamps, food rations, drinking water, explosives and sabotage equipment.

Had the Germans come, these units, operating behind enemy lines, would have tried to harry their advancing columns and to cut them off from supplies. They received their first training in the homes of the patrol leaders and then in the underground hideouts, followed by active combat sessions at the headquarters in Berkshire. They were never known as anything other than "Auxiliary Units".

David Lampe, who brilliantly researched this difficult area, was able to identify some of the key men in this operation, although no official lists were ever kept. Lampe's list, which refers specifically to 1941 but is likely to present an accurate picture of the position from the formation of the force, provides this information:

Light reconnaisance tanks passing through Linton, Cambridgeshire, during an Eastern Command exercise during August.   *Imperial War Museum*   ▶

Norfolk. Intelligence Office, Captain N. V. Oxenden, V.C.
Headquarters, Beeston Hall, near Neatishead.
Strength, 11 group commanders, 35 patrols, 201 men.
Hideouts (in 1941), 40.

Suffolk. Intelligence Officer, Captain J. W. Holberton.
Headquarters, Mill House, Cransford, near Woodbridge.
Strength, 5 group commanders, 28 patrols, 180 men.
Hideouts (in 1941), 28.

Essex. Intelligence Office, Captain R. F. H. Darwall Smith.
Headquarters, River House, Earls Colne.
Strength, 5 group commanders, 28 patrols, 169 men.
Hideouts (in 1941), 24.

The secrecy of the whole operation meant that few people were ever
aware of the siting of the hideouts. Only one appears to have been positively
identified and that was at Weeley, between Colchester and Clacton. It was
built of brick, concrete and steel, was well equipped to support a unit for a
month, and was served by a "letterbox" in a drainpipe at Frating, a village a
few miles away. [20]

If an invasion had occurred, Britain would have had to rely heavily on the Navy to batter or destroy the landing craft before they were beached. The Admiralty had over 700 armed patrol vessels, of which between two and three hundred were at sea at any one time between the Wash and Dover. In May and June many more trawlers and drifters were commandeered to form the Auxiliary Patrol, which now began to keep a watch close off-shore, in case invasion vessels slipped through the main patrol force further out. If invasion were attempted, the Navy advised that no more than 24 hours notice could ever be assured.

The British minefields in the North Sea were extended. Naval mine-sweepers and trawlers converted for minesweeping stepped up their efforts to keep the shipping lanes clear. Booms were erected across the estuary at Harwich and across the mouth of the Wash, the latter some five miles in length and complemented by a new minefield. One hundred miles of coastline in between was protected by a simple floating boom — wire nets hung from floating canvas tubes filled with kapok, and an alternative form of protection was provided by mines attached to wire jack-stays. [21]   Later in the summer these offshore barriers were replaced by a fence of builders' steel scaffolding, laced with barbed wire and sewn with mines, erected just below high water mark on the beaches. Practically all beaches were declared prohibited areas so far as the public was concerned.

Harwich was now one of the country's most important naval bases. By the beginning of July nine destroyers were based there; by the end of that month there were eighteen; soon afterwards the naval force was brought up to 22 destroyers and five corvettes, as well as the heavy cruiser HMS *Birmingham*. In face of the invasion threat, risks were taken elsewhere. Destroyers were desperately needed to protect merchant shipping in the Western Approaches, but heavy losses there were accepted as the lesser of two evils. [22]

The east coast ports were relatively well defended by the end of July. Harwich had seventeen heavy anti-aircraft guns, a good deal of smaller weaponry, and its balloon barrage. Comprehensive plans were finalised to deny these ports to the enemy, including mines and demolition charges and sunken blockships. The scores and ravines at Lowestoft were comprehensively mined, and they could be detonated in an emergency from the commodore's office.

Yet, when all these preparations were well under way, the Naval Staff informed Winston Churchill on July 12th: "It appears probable that a total of some 100,000 men might reach these shores without being intercepted by naval forces." The paper reviewed the probable landing places. It concluded that 50,000 German troops sailing from home ports might get ashore between Rosyth and Southwold, and 12,000 sailing from Dutch and Belgian ports might land between the Wash and Dover.

One of the many mobile rapid-firing A.A. guns, manned and escorted by sailors, which operated in the Harwich area.   *Imperial War Museum*

So what might the Royal Air Force be able to do to help? In May 1940 it had available 700 first-line fighters, of which 600 were Hurricanes and Spitfires, while the Germans were thought to have at least twice as many fighters and 3,000 bombers and dive-bombers. Great efforts were made during May to build up strength in the air. Coltishall, which had been under construction since early 1939 as an intended bomber base was now designated a fighter station. Before May was out No 66 Squadron of Fighter Command, one of the first squadrons to fly Spitfires, moved in. Horsham St Faith, which had been unused for some months, now accepted No 264 Squadron, the first to be equipped with the Boulton Paul Defiant fighter, which had just been passed for combat. At the airfield at Bottisham, near Cambridge, a few tents were erected as living quarters and Tiger Moth biplanes from the Cambridge Aero Club were flown in, to have 20-lb bombs strung from their fuselages. It was a measure of how desperate the situation then seemed.

One of several raiders shot down when German bombers attacked the Eastern Counties on 19th June.

B.B.C. Hulton Picture Library

During June a number of East Anglian aerodromes received the battered remnants of squadrons which had served in France before Dunkirk, and efforts began to rebuild them. Satellite airfields, with tented accommodation, were opened at Fowlmere (for Duxford) and Castle Camps (for Debden).

Bomber Command had new tasks to perform. From mid-May squadrons of Wellingtons flew from Feltwell, Honington and Marham to attack targets in Norway, the Netherlands and Germany. In June the Feltwell squadron was part of a force which sought to set the Black Forest ablaze by dropping phosphorous strips. By contrast, they made a flight to drop tea and sweets for children in Holland.

Immediately after Dunkirk, the Luftwaffe began a more sustained aerial attack on Britain. Their main targets were aerodromes — thirteen were raided during June — but no great damage was done at this stage. The first raid on Cambridgeshire was on June 6th, when the intended target was either Duxford or Fowlmere, but one hundred incendiary bombs were scattered around the village of Thriplow. Early during the morning of June 23rd bombs fell around the aerodrome at Marham — the first of many light attacks. On the 25th Debden was bombed for the first time, but escaped serious damage.

The first town in England to report a serious bombing raid was Cambridge. At midnight on June 19th the sirens wailed and fifteen minutes later a single Heinkel bomber swooped low over Gwydir Street — so low that its black outline was seen against the sky. It released two 550 lbs bombs, presumably aiming for the railway line, but they fell on modest terrace homes and blasted six of them, and a corner sweetshop, to rubble. Nine people were killed, including an evacuee schoolgirl from London, and nine more injured. One of the bombs fell only twenty yards from St Matthew's Church, but there was not so much as a cracked window there.

Not long afterwards a bomber was picked up by searchlights south of Cambridge and fighter planes closed in on it. Watchers saw the raider burst into flames and plummet to earth between Fulbourn and Balsham. In a searchlight beam one of the crew was seen floating down and he and his companions were soon rounded up and made prisoners by three men of the Babraham Home Guard: Privates Barnes, Wagstaff and Few senior. These may well have been the first prisoners taken anywhere by Home Guards.

Ipswich had its first raid twenty minutes after midnight on June 22nd, when ten high explosive bombs fell with a wierd whistling noise. Five failed to explode, but one which fell on a house in Dale Hall Lane caused the death of a married couple and their maidservant. The sirens now began to wail regularly in most parts of East Anglia, and bombs fell at various points in West Suffolk, in some rural parts of Norfolk, and almost all the way along the east coast, some of them at Felixstowe, Southwold and in the Lowestoft-Yarmouth area.

By July, light and widely scattered attacks were made almost every night, and during daylight single bombers or small formations began to penetrate inland. A Dornier bomber was shot down by A.A. guns when it attacked Harwich on July 1st. During the afternoon of July 3rd a raider dived almost to the rooftops in the centre of Lowestoft and released its bombs. One hit the main Co-operative Stores and started a fierce fire, which left only one wing of the building intact. Another demolished two working-class cottages, killing a nine-months-old baby in its pram, and its grandmother. A third damaged the Technical Institute. Anti-aircraft guns put up a heavy barrage and shells burst all around the plane, but it escaped, leaving four dead and 27 injured in the town. The same day twenty H.E. bombs were dropped on Ipswich; one woman was killed. Ipswich was a target again five days later, when ten bombs fell in the port area; three fell harmlessly into the water, and the others all failed to explode.

Then came the first attack on Norwich. At 5 p.m. on a warm summer afternoon, just as the workers were leaving the factories, two bombers flew in over the city at 600 feet. Their first bombs exploded on Barnards factory at Mousehold, where two men working on a loading dock were killed. The next bomb exploded on the top of Carrow Hill and the blast killed a number of workers, some of them women, who were pushing their bicycles up the hill from the factory gates. Four bombs then landed squarely on the Riverside factory of Boulton and Paul, where ten workers were killed and many injured. As dust and smoke billowed into the sky, more bombs were exploding on the railway tracks outside Thorpe station, several people were killed. The final toll in this raid, which was all over in a few minutes, was 27 dead and several dozen injured.

This attack, on July 9th, followed a few hours after a raid on Sprowston, where five people were killed — the first fatal air raid casualties in Norfolk.

The hazard of crashing planes continued throughout this period. An R.A.F. Hampden bomber fouled a cable of a barrage balloon at Harwich on June 13th and crashed on to a silo at Marriage's Flour Mill. There were several explosions and flames engulfed bomber, flour mill and a number of barges and rail trucks. The five R.A.F. crew and one civilian were killed.

Public behaviour in these early raids varied considerably. Many people went to their dugouts and shelters, as they had been advised to do, or at least left their beds and sat beneath the stairs. A lady living in a large house north of Chelmsford confided to her diary on June 18th:

> "A real tremor of shock goes through the house at 11 p.m. There is a lot of gunfire, bombs, some way off. Once a shout from the road. I cannot keep awake, yet a feeling of exhilaration that at last war is come here, too, that we are sharing, and a distinct warlikeness that is perhaps primitive — a desire to fight and to kill. Now and again between sleep the sound of a noisy low-flying Heinkel over our heads turns the stomach."

The next day the lady recorded that the Heinkel had crashed two miles away, "the three airmen shot to pieces and burned". A week later, after a day spent out-of-doors, the lady soliloquizes:

> "One enjoys little things extraordinarily. Lunch on a common, lying on ferns. One sucks the small minute dry, in gratitude." [23]

A quite different attitude was expressed by a farm worker interviewed by a Mass Observation representative after a plane had crashed near Eyke, in East Suffolk:

> "They never ought to have been invented, them bloody things. If everyone stayed in their own country, there'd be none of this trouble. There must be an awful lot of dead people out there, piles of them, German or British, it don't make no difference. There's one thing which ought to happen and stop all this. There ought to be an earthquake in France and swallow the whole bloody lot up, guns, men, tanks and all. That's the only way to stop war. There'll never be no end till they stop having armies. No one wants to fight. They all 'ave to go now. We all ought to stay at home and do nothing; that'd stop it." [24]

100

When there seemed a real possibility of an invasion attempt, the relations between the military authorities and the Regional Commissioner's organisation at Cambridge came under strain. Immediately after Dunkirk, Lieut. General H.R.S. Massy, Commander of the II Corps in East Anglia, despatched instructions from his headquarters at Hertford Barracks to each of his divisional commanders. This document, in conjunction with a small printed booklet which was sent out by the War Office at about the same time, caused some confusion as to what the military could or could not do. It implied that, in certain circumstances, a civilian offender detained by the Army might be brought before a military court for sentence. The Regional Commissioner's office challenged this suggestion. In fact, the government had already set up special "War Zone Courts" and in East Anglia two judges were available to travel immediately by police car to any area where a suspect had been detained. Trials were to take place in the market town nearest to, but outside, the fighting area in which the arrest had been made. An argument, conducted with great politeness, continued between members of the staffs of the Corps Commander and the Regional Commissioner until after the invasion crisis has passed. (25)

On June 8th the Deputy Regional Commissioner, the Earl of Cranbrook, sent a memorandum to Sir Will Spens which began:

"In the past there has been considerable trouble caused by junior and relatively junior Army officers taking it upon themselves to flood marshes, mine roads, fix tank traps, etc. without consultation, either with their superior officers or with the civil authorities."

At this time the military were urging that a large part of East Anglia should be declared a Defence Area, from which everyone except a minimum of essential workers should be evacuated. There was even a suggestion that martial law should be declared. On June 10th Sir Will Spens went to London to see Sir John Anderson, the Minister of Home Security; afterwards he wrote to General Massy reporting that he had raised the possibility of martial law over an area which would be large enough to include the inland aerodromes. Anderson had agreed that the coastal region should be declared a Defence Area and, according to Spens, had promised to put to the Cabinet a proposal for compulsory evacuation—but it was "by no means certain Cabinet will approve".

On June 13th General Ironside, C-in-C, Home Forces, expressed his view that martial law was unnecessary, commenting: "In the event of invasion by sea or air, the military authorities have such powers as military needs and the general situation requires, without any declaration of martial law." The C-in-C at the same time reminded his commanders in the field: "Regional Commissioners will continue to function in the event of invasion."

Bomb damage at Cemetry Road after an air-raid on Ipswich.   *G. Davis*

On June 17th the Minister signed an Order creating a Defence Area covering the whole of the coastal belt and including the towns of Wisbech, March, King's Lynn, Norwich, Great Yarmouth, Diss, Lowestoft, Ipswich, Stowmarket, Sudbury, Colchester, Braintree, Halstead, Chelmsford and Southend. Three times in a fortnight the War Cabinet considered the request that all but essential workers should be evacuated, and each time they rejected it. All that happened was that the Regional Commissioner issued a notice banning holiday-makers, after June 21st, from an area extending twenty miles inland from the coast between the Wash and the Thames. Anyone with "legitimate business' was permitted to enter the area; there was no system of passes, but anyone who went had to be prepared to satisfy military or police about their reasons for being there. The Regional Commissioner's office was called upon to adjudicate in some cases, as when a Norfolk girl living and working outside the Defence Area went home to visit her parents and took her boy friend with her. A police sergeant told them they must leave at once. There was a subsequent phone call from the Regional Commissioner's office to the Norfolk Police headquarters, after which the file was marked to indicate that any repetition was unlikely. Later there was the question whether gentlemen sportsmen should be admitted for the shoots on the big estates; it was agreed that they should.

W.A.A.F.s relaxing after a recruiting drive in Norfolk. *Eastern Daily Press*

It is certain that the Army would have preferred a tougher approach. After General Massy had made a visit to coastal Essex one morning, he dashed off a note to Spens: "Today I was at South Benfleet station and large parties arrived at about 10 a.m., obviously out for the day, with lunch baskets." He called for a more careful check of passengers on trains entering the Defence Area. A full police investigation which followed established that the day trippers were on their way to bungalows they owned on Canvey Island.

General Massy indicated to the Regional Commissioner on June 11th that he wished to have all livestock evacuated from farms in the coastal area immediately, and this movement began soon afterwards. It was decided that farm machinery, other than vans and lorries, could be retained, as it was needed for the coming harvest and "as it is contemplated that the enemy would be rapidly disposed of". But the military insisted that if invasion did take place, threatening areas inland, then "no attempt should be made to evacuate livestock . . . all livestock should be slaughtered to prevent their falling into the hands of the enemy."

While awaiting the government's decision whether East Anglia should be declared a Defence Area, General Massy sent Spens a memorandum on June 16th:

"If and when your Region or a portion of it is declared a Defence Area, I should be glad if all or as many as possible of the following courses of action could be undertaken:

a) Internment of all enemy aliens of whatever category in the area;
b) Removal from the area of all British subjects of alien extraction, including nationals of Southern Ireland;
c) Internment of all members of the British Fascist organisation;
d) Removal from the area of all members of the Peace Pledge Union;
e) Prohibition of entry into the area of all non-residents other than officials who must have a special pass . . .
f) Removal of all pleasure craft from the coast and the inland waterways, including the Norfolk Broads;
g) Control under special licence of all other river craft;
h) A curfew between 2200 and 0500 daily, particularly for motor and bicycle traffic, if we cannot get the complete curfew. Doctors, etc. would require special police passes."

The Regional Commissioner, in reply, promised to press in the first instance for the items (a), (f) and (h), but it was some time before action followed. Eventually Spens issued an order that, after midnight on July 9th, no private car might use any road within five miles of the towns of Great Yarmouth, Lowestoft, Southwold, Aldeburgh, Felixstowe, Harwich, Frinton and Walton, Clacton and Southend, unless they held a special permit. Cars without a permit had either to be removed from the area altogether or effectively immobilised. In the latter case, parts removed from vehicles had to be handed over to the police and they were sent away to a special store at Bedford. During the remainder of 1940, at least, any owner who moved elsewhere or who sold his vehicle found that it was impossible to reclaim the missing parts from store.

Spens' next order, effective from July 12th, required that all small craft be immobilised. They had to be taken from the water and removed to a distance inland. On July 28th came an order imposing a curfew from one hour after sunset until one hour before sunrise in a five-miles-wide coastal strip from north to south of the region. Towns and villages were excluded, as was traffic on A or B main roads.

In the midst of the consideration of these difficult matters, Sir Will Spens received a visit from General Ironside, C-in-C of Home Forces, who afterwards recorded his impressions thus:

"I dined in Corpus Christi with Will Spens. A real old Fifeshire accent. A most efficient Regional Commissioner. I had a long talk with him. He told me that there were many intellectuals who were already defeatists. I cannot imagine such a mentality.

His own attitude was that he hoped the government was not continuing out of pride or fear of telling the House that there was no chance.

I told him that the war had not yet begun. That the history of Napoleon was being repeated and that we need have no fear if we had stout hearts. That I knew we could defeat the Germans, given stout hearts.

He agreed. He then tackled me about the people 'staying put' in case of an invasion. He had it on his conscience that we were arranging sabotage behind the lines if the Germans succeeded in landing. He wanted it stopped. A most upright attitude, I thought, but treating the Germans as if they were civilised beings . . ."*(26)

While discussion took place in high places about what should be done about civilians living near the coast, the people concerned became increasingly apprehensive. Bunty Carr noted in her diary on June 18th:

"Mother and Jenny packed a bag each of essential things. I suggested that mother is so unnerved that she and Jenny go somewhere on the west coast, starting at 8 a.m. tomorrow, with the dog, but when it comes to the point they will not go . . ."

Sister Jenny, in her diary, adds the bizarre footnote:

"I can't make up my mind whether to wear my winter or summer coat if I have to flee, as I like them both."

On July 5th Winston Churchill sought to clarify the government's attitude in a memorandum circulated to staff:

"Clear instructions should now be issued about the people living in the threatened coastal zones: They should be encouraged as much as possible to depart voluntarily, both by the pressure of a potential compulsory order hanging over them, and also by local (not national) propaganda through their Regional Commissioners or local bodies.

Those who wish to stay, or can find nowhere to go on their own, should be told that if invasion impact occurs in their town or village on the coast they will not be able to leave till the battle is over. They should, therefore, be encouraged and helped to put their cellars in order so that they have fairly safe places to go to . . . Only those who are trustworthy should be allowed to stay. All doubtful elements should be removed . . ."

Householders who left were freed, by government decree, from liability to pay rent, rates, or water, gas, electricity or telephone charges in respect of homes which had been locked up and evacuated. By mid-July 127,000 people, nearly half the population, had left the East Anglian coast towns. (27)

* The Lord Ironside.

CHAPTER SEVEN

The Battle of Britain

AT 4.40 a.m. on July 10th three Spitfires of No 66 Squadron took off from Coltishall, the newly commissioned aerodrome eight miles north of Norwich, and climbed to 15,000 feet. Over Stalham they encountered a lone Dornier bomber. It was above them and as they climbed astern of it a German gunner raked one of the Spitfires with bullets and forced it to disengage. The other two pressed home their attack as the Dornier turned for home and eventually they shot it down in the sea; they saw three of the crew swimming in the water before they left the scene. Only minutes later, several German planes swooped down on Martlesham aerodrome, near Ipswich, and dropped eighteen high explosive bombs along the edge of the airfield, but without causing damage or casualties.

These were the first events in the air on the day which has come to be accepted as the start of the Battle of Britain.

It was in the air that that battle was to be fought and won, although no-one could have known it at the time. Its first phase, which lasted from July 10th to August 12th, was intended by the Germans to destroy Britain's naval strength; their attack was concentrated on ports and shipping. The second phase, between August 13th to September 15th, aimed to destroy the air defence of Britain; sustained assault took place on R.A.F. Fighter Command aerodromes, on radar stations and on factories manufacturing aircraft. Until these two objectives had been achieved the German army could not invade.

A Hawker Hurricane in Battle of Britain colours. *Kinsey*

Most people in East Anglia had learnt by this time to identify the two fighter planes which were to prove the instruments of victory, the Hawker Hurricane and the Spitfire. The Hurricane, which had been developed during the 'thirties, was credited with four-fifths of all enemy aircraft destroyed, once the battle was over and the score was calculated. They were single-seater planes with a maximum speed of 316 m.p.h. and an armament of eight machine-guns, and they formed two-thirds of the R.A.F's modern fighter strength when the battle began. Spitfires formed the remaining third. The first of them had been delivered to Duxford just a year before the war began and their speed—maximum of 355 m.p.h.—and outstanding handling qualities made them popular with pilots. The design of this most famous of all British fighters was one of the greatest achievements of Reginald J. Mitchell, much of whose work on high speed flight in the inter-war years was done in Felixstowe.

In the summer of 1940 all the newspapers published outline diagrams and basic information about the Luftwaffe aircraft which began to appear overhead each day. There was the Messerschmidt 109 figher, which had fought in earlier campaigns in Spain and Poland and which now showed itself to be operationally the equal of the Spitfire. But it could fly for only ninety minutes without refuelling, so that anywhere north of the Thames it was operating its extreme limits and had often to break off in the middle of an encounter to make for base. There was the Messerschmidt 110 fighter-bomber, the primary purpose of which to cut a path through enemy defences so that the heavy bombers could come through. These planes were used during the battle for a number of hit-and-run raids on R.A.F. aerodromes in East Anglia.

The Supermarine Spitfire 1, the standard type, with three-bladed variable pitch airscrew, used during the Battle of Britain. *Kinsey*

As for the bombers, the Junkers 87, the "Stuka" dive-bomber which spread terror in Spain, Poland and Belgium, was not much used against England, for it proved very vulnerable to modern R.A.F. fighters. The twin-engined Junkers 88, on the other hand, was an effective and versatile aircraft which could be used for every kind of bombing operation, for mine laying, and even as a night fighter. Heinkel 111s and Dornier 17s, each of which carried 2,200 lbs bomb-loads, were the most frequently seen over England.

There was, by July 1940, a highly sophisticated defence system to deal with the threat presented by this powerful German air force. R.A.F. Fighter Command had divided Britain into four areas, each of which formed a Group Command. The air space over East Anglia was the responsibility of two different Groups. No 11 Group, which was commanded by Air Vice Marshall Keith Park from headquarters at Uxbridge, operated below a line drawn from Great Yarmouth on the coast to a point some miles south of Cambridge, and thus included the aerodromes at Debden, Martlesham Heath and North Weald. No 12 Group, commanded by Air Vice Marshal Trafford Leigh-Mallory from headquarters near Nottingham, included most of Norfolk, Suffolk and Cambridgeshire, and thus embraced the bases at Duxford and Fowlmere, Coltishall and Horsham St Faith.

Each Group was divided into sectors: there were seven in No 11 Group (of which Debden and North Weald were those principally concerned with beating off raids approaching over Essex, from the North Sea) and six in No 12 Group. Sector stations normally handled three squadrons, and the normal establishment of a fighter squadron was 26 pilots and sixteen aircraft, with a few others in reserve. None of the bases in East Anglia was up to this strength when the Battle of Britain began. Duxford had two squadrons with a dozen Hurricanes and Spitfires and a dozen Defiants, which was a much less satisfactory fighter plane. Coltishall had two squadrons with 24 Hurricanes and Spitfires, and this was also the strength at Debden and at North Weald. Once airborne, pilots were guided into battle from sector "Operations Rooms".

The Operations Rooms received intelligence about enemy aircraft movements from the network of radar stations around the coast and from nearly 50,000 men, women and youths who gave voluntary service in the Observer Corps. This information was coordinated and analysed and displayed visually, so that the position of attacking forces at any moment was clear, and R.A.F. fighter pilots could be kept fully briefed.

The radar system had been perfected, and a string of stations erected, only just in time to be effective when the air war began and, without it, the Luftwaffe's numerical superiority might have been decisive. By the summer of 1940, however, radar screens plainly showed the German bombing fleets as

The Operations Room at R.A.F. Fighter Station, Duxford, during 1940.   *Imperial War Museum*

they were leaving their airfields across the Channel, and continued to track them though they sought cloud cover. Their position, height and bearing — even an estimate of the number of aircraft — was passed by telephone to the R.A.F. Operations Rooms.

When raiders crossed the English coast, the Observer Corps took over and plotted their tracks inland, similarly telephoning information to the R.A.F. There were about fifty Observer Posts in each R.A.F. Group area, arranged in clusters of three or four, and they were manned around the clock. They were responsible to Observer Centres located at Norwich, Bury St Edmunds, Cambridge and Colchester. An *Eastern Daily Press* reporter who visited an Observer Post in Norfolk described it thus:

> "It is an unroofed enclosure of corrugated iron, eight feet square, manned by a crew of two who, apart from partial shelter afforded by a connecting dugout, have to carry out their duties exposed to all types of weather.
>
> One wears headphones linking him with the control centre and the other stands watching and listening. In front of them is a circular table marked off in a series of numbered squares and pivoted on its centre is a revolving instrument by means of which they are able to sight and plot the course of the object overhead . . .

Thus the Observers are able to track the position of any aircraft from the time it enters their area until it leaves, the information is simultaneously passed on by telephone and the next post is ready to take similar action. Flying heights are also estimated and checked." (1)

Throughout the No 11 Group area there were searchlights at intervals of about 6,000 yards, but they were more closely sited along the coast and in those areas which had heavy anti-aircraft guns; here the distance between them was about 3,500 yards. The 6th A.A. Division, the responsibilities of which coincided with No 11 Group area, had 37 heavy A.A. guns, 101 light A.A. guns, 437 Lewis and Hispano machine guns at aerodromes and other vital points. Each searchlight site had its own machine gun for use against low-flying aircraft and for ground defence. (2)

This was the air defence organisation which Germany was now determined to destroy. Hoping to kill two birds at once, the early attacks were made on shipping and coastal targets; if R.A.F. fighters could be drawn up in their defence, the Luftwaffe hoped to take toll of both ships and planes.

On July 11th a Dornier sent out to report on weather conditions over the Suffolk and Norfolk coast was intercepted off Great Yarmouth just after dawn by three Spitfires from Coltishall. It eluded them, but very soon afterwards met a lone Hurricane flown by the legless pilot Douglas Bader, who had just been given command of No 242 Squadron at Coltishall. This was one of six Hurricane squadrons which had returned from France, utterly exhausted, less than a month before, and Bader had the task of building it up again. This early July morning he showed the spirit which was to make his name a legend, and the Dornier went diving into the sea off Cromer.

Squadron Leader Peter Townsend, flying a similar lone dawn patrol in a Hurricane from Martlesham, was less fortunate when he encountered a Dornier off Harwich the same day. He came off worst in the fight that followed, had to bale out, and was picked up by a naval launch after twenty minutes in the sea. Later that day, German planes bombed Cromer, Yarmouth and Ipswich.

On July 12th there was a heavy attack on a convoy, codenamed *Booty*, while it was steaming southward off Orfordness. Dorniers and Heinkels dived out of the clouds at breakfast-time and showered down bombs. The vessels in the convoy passed unscathed, but a fierce aerial battle took place. Hurricanes from Debden which had been accompanying the convoy shot down two Heinkels and one Dornier, and a second Dornier was claimed by Hurricanes sent from North Weald. A third squadron of Hurricanes, from Martlesham, also joined in the fray. Two Hurricane pilots, one from Martlesham and one from North Weald, lost their lives when their planes were shot down.

Within the following week it became noticeable that the main weight of the German attack moved to the English Channel and the south coast, although the North Sea shipping and the east coast also took punishment. The explanation—though it was not known at the time—was the "Directive No 16" issued by Hitler on July 16th:

> "As England, in spite of the hopelessness of her military position, has so far shown herself unwilling to come to any compromise, I have decided to begin to prepare for, and if necessary to carry out, an invasion of England . . . if necessary, the island will be occupied."

Hitler's proposal was for "a surprise crossing on a broad front extending approximately from Ramsgate to a point west of the Isle of Wight", but even the German troops in Holland were encouraged to think that there might still be an invasion of the east coast between the Wash and Harwich, and certainly that possibility was still uppermost in the minds of British defence chiefs. Air activity in this sector continued day by day. On July 21st six bombs missed the Sparrow's Nest at Lowestoft and exploded in the sea. On the 26th small Luftwaffe formations attacked North Sea convoys and heavy bombs from a Heinkel sank the destroyer HMS *Wren* (1,120 tons) off Aldeburgh. Three Junkers were shot down along the coast in ten days, one at St Osyth, one off Yarmouth and one off Happisburgh.

Single planes continued to fly inland from time to time. Norwich was bombed on July 19th and 30th, and on August 1st and 10th, and about two dozen people were killed. A Junkers plane crashed at Bury St Edmunds at midnight on July 30th after catching fire in mid-air. A Heinkel bomber crashed in the garden of Bishopscourt, the home of the Bishop of Chelmsford, and the Bishop conducted the funeral service of the three crewmen who were killed. The fourth German, injured, parachuted down near Writtle, where he knocked on a cottage door to awaken the occupant, and was glad to be arrested soon afterwards by the local constable. [3]

On August 1st six Junkers dive-bombed a convoy off Norfolk, but three Hurricanes from Coltishall attacked and shot one into the sea. In a raid on a convoy the following day one of the trawlers requisitioned by the Navy, *Cape Finisterre* (590 tons), was sunk and on August 4th and 5th two other requisitioned trawlers were sunk by mines: *Drummer* (297 tons) off Brightlingsea, and *River Clyde* (276 tons) off Aldeburgh. On August 11th eight Dorniers, accompanied by twenty Messerschmidt fighters, arrived over a convoy off the Harwich - Clacton shore at 11.50 a.m. but met half-a-dozen R.A.F. Hurricanes which were covering the convoy and eleven Spitfires which quickly arrived as reinforcements. In a fierce battle, four Messerschmidts were shot down and three Dorniers damaged, for the loss of two Hurricanes. The fight was resumed about fifteen minutes later over Clacton, when one Junkers was shot down and a second damaged, and the R.A.F. lost two Spitfires, both of whose pilots died. On the same day two Messerschmidts were shot down off Harwich after they had taken part in an attack on Martlesham aerodrome.

An observer post near Hadleigh in 1940.   *Suffolk Record Office*

By this time Goering had taken personal command of the assault on Britain. He told a conference of fleet commanders in Berlin that the invasion would be launched in the second week of September, and he fixed an Adler Tag (Eagle Day) on which would be launched the decisive air attack that would destroy the R.A.F. After a postponement because of weather, this attack came on August 13th, and it was the southeastern corner of England which took the full force of it.

On the 15th, however, the Germans launched what was planned as a "massive synchronised assault on Britain that was timed to saturate the defences over an 800-mile front, from Edinburgh to Exeter", with the Fighter Command airfields as primary targets. [4] Raid No 22, in the German orders of the day, was on Martlesham aerodrome and it took place simultaneously with other big attacks on bases all over eastern and southern England. Sixteen Messerschmidt 110 fighter-bombers, accompanied by nine Messerschmidt 109 fighters, carried out a precision hit-and-run raid which was all over in four and a half minutes and which put the aerodrome out of operation for 48 hours. It began with cannon and machine-gun fire, and then the raiders aimed about 30 bombs. A Fairey Battle bomber on the ground caught fire and the 1,000 lbs of bombs with which it was laden exploded with such violence that two hangars were badly damaged, the watch tower demolished, and much other damage caused. The German bombs cut the water and telephone services and damaged the officers' mess and the workshops. The Germans suffered no losses and when they were intercepted south of Harwich, on their way back to France, they shot down five R.A.F. Hurricanes.

August 15th saw the most bitter fighting of the whole Battle of Britain. The Luftwaffe launched five massive assaults, using 1,790 planes and flying 2,000 sorties. Fighter Command flew nearly 1,000 sorties. By nightfall, the Germans had lost 90 planes and the R.A.F. 42, and Britain's air defences had survived.

After this the assault on airfields continued relentlessly, day after day until mid-September. Huge bomber formations, with fighter support, were hurled across the Channel and the objective was nothing less than to blast the aerodromes so thoroughly that the R.A.F. would be forced to abandon them. All the bases had been provided with elaborate decoys at some miles distance, with landing lights and, in some cases, dummy planes which had been turned out of the props department of the film studios at Shepperton. These sometimes served very well, as on August 16th, when 220 high explosive bombs were dropped not far from Duxford without causing any significant damage.

The main weight of the attack continued to fall south of the Thames, but some of the fiercest air battles were fought over the eastern counties, where most of the aerodromes were raided. On August 18th four Heinkel bombers in a force sent to attack North Weald were shot down — three into the sea and the

EAST ANGLIA 1940

fourth at Foulness; a Messerschmidt 110 crashed and burnt out in sandpits at Clacton; and two Hurricanes crashed after a dogfight over Chelmsford. By this time Fighter Command was under considerable strain. In ten days it had lost 154 pilots, killed, missing or badly wounded, and 213 fighter planes. In the same period only 63 new pilots had come forward from training units to join the squadrons and fewer than 150 Hurricanes and Spitfires had left the factories. [5]   A letter written by a pilot officer flying on convoy patrol from Martlesham gave a glimpse of conditions: "We start at 4.30 a.m. and go on until 9.30 p.m., with about 35 minutes off for each meal." It was at this stage that Winston Churchill delivered to Parliament his memorable tribute to the fighter pilots: "Never in the field of human conflict was so much owed by so many to so few."

Heinkel HE 111 H-3 of the type which operated from France against the British Isles during 1940. *Kinsey*

The bomber base at Honington and the fighter station at Coltishall were attacked on August 19th. One of the Dorniers flying back from Honington was shot down into the sea off Great Yarmouth; a Spitfire from Coltishall suffered a similar fate off Orfordness and the Aldeburgh lifeboat went out to pick up the pilot, who failed to regain consciousness. That score was evened the following day when a Coltishall Hurricane destroyed a Messerschmidt off Aldeburgh. The Luftwaffe hit Martlesham again.

On the 21st Coltishall and Horsham St Faiths were attacked. The Germans lost five Dorniers, one of which crashed in Gippeswyk Park at Ipswich, a second at Starston, in the Waveney Valley, two near Mablethorpe, and the other north of Burnham Market. In the first raid on Coltishall six H.E. bombs were dropped on a new and uncompleted hangar on which about a hundred men were working, and a number of them were killed. When the Luftwaffe returned two days later:

114

"It was like disturbing a hornet's nest. Both squadrons shot up and then began a lovely game of hide-and-seek in and out of the clouds over the camp. Presently, one of our Hurricanes came back full out, dived down low over the 'drome and shot up into the air again, doing a complete roll. That's the sign they all give if they have scored a victory." [6]

Debden aerodrome was seriously damaged in two raids at the end of the month. More than a hundred high explosive and incendiary bombs were dropped on each occasion, and with remarkable accuracy. There were direct hits on the landing area, the parade ground, the motor transport yard, the equipment stores, a barracks block, the sick quarters, the Women's Auxiliary Air Force quarters, the sergeants' mess, the NAAFI and the cookhouse. Electricity and water mains were damaged. Four R.A.F. men and one civilian were killed. The Operations Room had to be transferred from the aerodrome to a hut in a disused chalk-pit near Saffron Walden, where it functioned until the gymnasium at Saffron Walden grammar school could be requisitioned for the purpose. But Debden was never again attacked in such strength.

The first of these two attacks was on August 26th and was accompanied by widespread aerial combat. Three Dornier bombers were shot down by the R.A.F. within ten minutes: one at Highams Farm, Thaxted, one at Wimbish, near Saffron Walden, and one near Clacton. Two Messerschmidt 110s were destroyed, crashing at Great Tey and Bentley, on either side of Colchester. Three Hurricanes were lost: two from Duxford crashed at Maldon and at Rumbolds Farm, Southminster, and one from Debden crashed and burnt out at Great Totham, near Maldon.

The pilots' rest room at R.A.F. Fighter Station, Duxford. *Imperial War Museum*

Before the second attack on Debden, there was a spectacular battle over Chelmsford on August 30th, when Hurricanes engaged a force of Heinkel bombers on their way home after bombing a target at Radlett. Six Heinkels and two Hurricanes came spinning from the sky. One of the Heinkels hit the ground near Hunsdon rectory and another at Colne Engaine. One of Hurricanes came down near Halstead.

August 31st was the day on which the East Anglian skies seemed to be ripped apart. Early that day radar stations reported a force of 200 German aircraft flying up the Thames estuary. Thirteen squadrons of R.A.F. fighters were scrambled from seven airfields. At 9 a.m. twelve Hurricanes from Martlesham attacked a force of about fifty Messerschmidt 110s head-on near Clacton. Each side lost two planes in the combat. Soon afterwards twelve Hurricanes from North Weald engaged a German formation over Colchester and were badly mauled; four of the R.A.F. planes were shot down without any return score. Next, nine Hurricanes from Debden intercepted a force of Dorniers making for Duxford aerodrome and attacked so resolutely that the Germans scattered and turned away from the target. They jettisoned 120 to 150 bombs in open country between Duxford and Cambridge, around the villages of Meldreth, Shepreth, Harston and Shelford. One Dornier, one Messerschmidt and one R.A.F. Hurricane were shot down in this engagement.

While a Debden squadron was thus protecting Duxford, its own station was getting its second bad beating within six days. Apart from the damage already described, four Hurricanes were badly damaged on the ground. It was difficult to keep count of the planes which fell stricken from the skies. Hurricanes crashed at Debden, at Halstead, near Colchester, on the foreshore at Walton, and in Colne Creek. Dorniers came down near Felixstowe, near Duxford and in rural Suffolk.

There was another tremendous battle over Colchester on September 3rd, when wave after wave of Hurricanes and Spitfires attacked a force of Dorniers making for home after a very damaging attack on North Weald aerodrome. The British fighters found themselves in a series of bitter dogfights with the accompanying Messerschmidt 110s. "The sky around Colchester was streaked with trails of stricken aircraft and mottled with parachutes." [7] One Dornier was shot down over the river Crouch, but the R.A.F. lost seven Hurricanes and two Spitfires.

The public was, of course, told nothing of this devastating German assault on the R.A.F. aerodromes and so their attention fastened on the relatively small-scale "nuisance raids" on the towns. Felixstowe was raided at early evening on August 16th, when the post office, a hotel, the Amusement Park and several shops and houses were damaged. A large number of incendiary bombs were rained around Herringfleet, just outside Lowestoft, late on the night of August 19th, causing damage to growing crops. Norwich was raided with incendiaries on the 20th, and Southwold with high explosives on the 20th and 21st. Lowestoft was grievously hit on the 21st when there was a direct hit on a public shelter, killing half a dozen people. A shipyard and a timber yard were also damaged. Cromer and Harwich were bombed on the 23rd and on that day, too, bombs jettisoned over Colchester caused many casualties. On the 28th eight H.E. bombs fell in and around Cambridge, but without causing casualties. One landed on Fenner's cricket pitch. On August 29th there were two damaging raids on Felixstowe; incendiaries caused a fire at the Pier Pavilion at dusk, and planes came back in the early hours of the morning to drop 54 H.E. bombs in the harbour area and on the railway. On September 4th Felixstowe was again attacked twice, during the evening. On September 11th the teatime calm of Eye, in Suffolk, was disturbed when a German plane appeared overhead and dropped three H.E. bombs. They all failed to explode and one of them bounced through the open window of a bedroom over a shop near the town hall. On September 14th a Junkers dive-bombed Ipswich during the afternoon. One bomb fell near St Margaret's Green and shattered some of the windows of the church, but a wedding service inside carried on without interruption.

This catalogue by no means covers all the enemy activity over East Anglia during the period. Bombs fell in very many places, some of which presented no worthwhile target, as single German planes ranged widely over the region. Sometimes they swooped down and machine-gunned people in the streets: a postman on his round, a lone cyclist on a country road, a queue at a bus-stop.

The big assault on the aerodromes reached its peak on August 31st and was then sustained for a full week. During this period there was a limited exchange of squadrons between aerodromes in East Anglia and those in the southeast, in order to give some relative relief to the exhausted pilots who were taking the brunt of the battle. Such exchanges took place between Castle Camps and Croydon, and between Coltishall and Kenley. Duxford was at the centre of a controversy which arose within Fighter Command. Air Vice Marshal Trafford Leigh-Mallory, who commanded No 12 Group, which included Duxford, produced what became known as the "Big Wing" concept. He argued that the massive formations of attackers should be met by large numbers of fighters operating as a single formation, rather than in individual squadrons. He transferred No 242 Squadron, commanded by Bader, from Coltishall to Duxford to join Nos 19 and 310 Squadrons there, and he authorised Bader to lead all three squadrons of Hurricanes as a wing. Later two more squadrons were added, so that by September 15th sixty Hurricanes and Spitfires were flying as a "Big Wing". It claimed some spectacular successes during the Battle of Britain, but the argument as to whether it was the best strategy was never really settled.

During the first seven days of September the R.A.F. suffered the virtual destruction of six squadrons. Between Goering's "Adler Tag" and September 6th it lost 401 planes. It was true that the Germans had lost 670, but they had begun the battle with an enormous superiority of numbers. For the R.A.F. "the strain was severe . . . Another week of such attacks might have been disastrous." [8]

The time had now come when the Germans, according to their earlier plans, would attempt a cross-Channel invasion and a landing on British shores. The R.A.F. had not been destroyed, which was a declared pre-requisite for that invasion, but a great concentration of invasion barges was taking place in the French ports. During the first week of September Wellingtons of Bomber Command, some of them from Marham in Norfolk, were sent each night to bomb them.

It was not until the end of the first week in August that General Brooke, who had by then succeeded General Ironside as C-in-C of Home Forces, advised that the invasion threat "was developing on the south coast as much as on the east". [9] A great deal of redeployment of troops then took place. The forces between the Wash and the Thames were reduced from seven divisions to four plus one armoured brigade, and the strength on the south coast was increased from five divisions to nine plus two armoured brigades. [10] The

Wing Commander (later Group Captain) D. R. S. Bader, D.S.O., D.F.C.

Kinsey

118

divisions in reserve were now moved forward into Cambridgeshire, Hertford-shire and Surrey, so that they were available to move either southward or eastward. Churchill's intention was that it should be possible to concentrate 10,000 men, fully equipped, within six hours, and 20,000 men within twelve hours at any point where the enemy gained a bridgehead. (11)

There was a new emphasis upon the construction of strong "nodal points" for all-round defence of important road junctions and communications centres. Each city and town now evolved its own special defence scheme, worked out by the local commander, in consultation with the Home Guard and field force officers. A great deal was entrusted to local decision-making. Many more pill-boxes were built, but the Home Guard was advised not to depend too heavily upon them. The Commander of the 55th Division, for example, circulated this order on August 6th:

> "Pill-boxes must be regarded as the keep of a section locality, in which the garrison (of six) can shelter during air attack by bombs or machine-guns. As soon as air attack ceases, the garrison must leave the pill-boxes and take post in trenches. All six must be able to fire. Each pill-box must have supporting fire trenches, A.A. slits, and Molotov Cocktail holes to give all-round defence." (12)

Guidance was sent out on all sorts of problems expected to arise when the invaders arrived. A recognition signal to be used between British ground troops was devised: "four distinct short hoots on a motor horn whistle or any other sound producer at approximately one second intervals." Advice on questioning suspected enemy agents was offered: "The following test words may help to discover the genuineness or otherwise of persons who ask the way or try to obtain information: *North Sea, clothes, wretch, tough, throat, those, soothe, wrong, buckle, trough, rats, through.*" (13)

Something almost approaching spy fever still prevailed, so that the Ministry of Home Security felt it necessary to circulate an appeal to police and wardens to do more to verify reports of suspects before passing them on. "The number of unsubstantiated reports of parachute landings which have reached the Home Security War Room is such as to be likely to cause serious dislocation to the War Room machinery in the event of genuine attempts by the Germans to land troops by planes or parachutes," it complained. (14)

It had been laid down early in the summer that if and when the time came that all British forces should be brought to battle stations, formal liaison established between military and civil administration, and civilian telephone and telegraph lines requisitioned for military use, the codeword "Cromwell" would be circulated. On the night of September 6th/7th the Admiralty ordered all cruisers, destroyers and small craft to be at immediate notice during darkness. Late in the afternoon of Saturday, September 7th the greatest air armada in history — 348 bombers accompanied by 617 fighters — crossed the coast of Kent and flew towards London. They unloaded their bombs on the capital, most of them on the docklands and East London, in what was to be the first of 57 consecutive nights of blitzkrieg.

The Chiefs of Staff were in session when the first reports came in and they went straight to No 10 Downing Street to see the Prime Minister. At seven minutes past eight that evening, as a second wave of bombers was arriving, the signal "Cromwell" was sent out to Home Forces. At 9.50 p.m. Fighter Command headquarters despatched to all stations an Alert No 1.

What followed must have proved disconcerting to a lot of people. For a start, the Cromwell signal took nearly four hours to reach troops on the coast, and the R.A.F. signal was not received at Martlesham until 5.20 a.m. the following morning and, because it was not marked "priority", it was not decoded until 10.30 a.m. [15] These may well have been exceptions. In Ipswich the Home Guard received orders to Stand To at 10.30 p.m. and the defence lines around the town were manned soon after midnight. It was more difficult in rural areas, because only a few of the Home Guard officers were on the telephone. "It was not so easy driving round and calling out platoon commanders in the dark," one commander in Cambridgeshire recalled later. Another, at Hauxton, noted:

> "Visited by Colonel Y--- at 11.5 p.m. and ordered to man action stations in readiness for the anticipated invasion. Runner to be permanently posted at police station. Personnel to proceed to work armed and in uniform. All defences at focal points, with blocks out, bombs, etc. in position." [16]

It was said afterwards that some enthusiastic Royal Engineers blew up bridges in East Anglia and laid mines which killed several Guards officers, and that church bells were rung in some places. [17] But no one was ready to admit to such errors and no records seem to have been kept. In one part of Norfolk it was explained that falling bombs had caused the church bells to vibrate!

On the following morning, and for several days afterwards, rumour ran rife. A diarist in Bury St Edmunds noted:

> "Tales beginning to come through about an attempted invasion last Saturday evening. All LDVs called out. Tales of how the enemy got to within six miles of our coast and were then sunk. Dead bodies on the beaches reported." [18]

The Germans, however, well knew that they had not achieved the conditions in which an invasion attempt stood any chance of success. And, by switching the weight of their attack to London just at the moment when the

Fighter Command stations were at the very limit of their endurance, they had taken the pressure off the Hurricane and Spitfire pilots. When, on Sunday, September 15th, Goering made a last, desperate effort to win the war in the air, these pilots were refreshed and their morale was high.

They smashed two major Luftwaffe assaults during the day. As 100 Dorniers, with accompanying fighters, came in sight of London during the morning they were simultaneously attacked by nine R.A.F. squadrons. Forty-three Hurricanes of four different squadrons met them head-on. The Duxford "Big Wing" led by Bader—three squadrons of Hurricanes and two of Spitfires—closed in on them from the flanks and hammered the escorting fighters. The formation of bombers disintegrated. There was a repeat performance during the afternoon. This time 150 Dorniers and Heinkels approached, flying in three formations. Again the Duxford wing fell upon them from the flanks, while eight other squadrons met them head-on, and again the attack was broken up completely.

At the end of that day the R.A.F. claimed 185 German planes destroyed, and that gave a tremendous boost to national morale. In fact, as was later established, the true figure of German losses was only about 60 planes—but that was quite sufficient to undermine the confidence of the enemy. Goering had now to accept that he could not destroy the R.A.F. Four days later Hitler called off the plan for an invasion in 1940 and in Britain the Cromwell alert was cancelled.

Winston Churchill, the Prime Minister, toured some of the East Coast defences in August. He is seen here inspecting men of the 2nd Battalion of the Cambridgeshire Regiment at Holt.   *Imperial War Museum*

CHAPTER EIGHT

The Home Front

IT WAS the strangest summer East Anglia has ever known. Every day people could pause in the street, look up, and watch one of the most decisive battles of world history being fought. Then they would continue on their way, to fields, factories and offices, and try to settle down to work normally; but not quite normally, for there was now a relentless pressure on everyone to increase their efficiency and to step up production. Stanley Ratcliff, a farmer at Maldon, gave this description:

> "We just carried on with our work on the farm. I remember one day in 1940 we were carting barley for the rick-yard, three men working on the stack and one unpitching from the waggon. The air overhead was full of planes and a great battle was going on, but the men never stopped work.
>
> Every now and then one of them would call out: 'Here comes another one down – that makes two'.
>
> 'There's a third'.
>
> But all the time unpitching sheaves of corn . . . The one man on the farm who gets no fun or excitement out of all this is the man who drives the tractor. He can't hear the warning or the planes and he has to look where he is going. He just can't help carrying on from dawn to dark, whether he likes it or not." [1]

The farmers gathered a good harvest from their greatly increased acres of arable land. The weather had not favoured them and the sugar beet crop, in particular, was a disappointment; on some farms the land had to be ploughed up after a second, or even a third, drilling had failed. On the other hand, the potato crop was exceptionally heavy everywhere. The Ministry of Food was quick off the mark with an "Eat more potatoes" campaign, and potatoes were used in brewing, to save barley. According to the East Anglian farmers, cereal yields were poor, but the government said they were above the pre-war average, although not as high as in 1939.

A new Minister of Agriculture, Mr R. S. Hudson, announced a revised government policy at the beginning of June, with improved farm prices, and a new scheme of grants for tile drainage, designed to encourage full production from maximum acreage. On the other hand, pig and poultry stock had to be reduced, to save imported feeding stuffs. The new policy also prescribed a minimum weekly wage of 48 shillings for farm employees, which the farmers declared would increase their costs, directly and indirectly, by about thirty per cent. The higher prices they received were supposed to take care of that.

Before the harvest of 1940 was gathered, the Ministry was discussing new ploughing quotas for each county. Until the ploughing began again, farmers were urged to place obstacles (or build haystacks) in the centre of their fields, to prevent aircraft landing. "Dig for Victory" posters were everywhere. A Ministry of Agriculture leaflet, issued during the period when invasion seemed imminent, declared:

"Farmers! Unless military action in the immediate neighbourhood makes it impossible, farmers and farm workers must go on ploughing, sowing, cultivating, hoeing and harvesting as though no invasion was occurring."

Farmers proved to be exceptionally resilient, and managed to maintain many of the main features of country life. The annual sales of ewes and lambs in July preserved their familiar atmosphere; over 3,000 were auctioned at Norwich and about 2,000 at Bury St Edmunds. But many changes were inevitable, and some of them were trying:

"It was no fun to be a farmer. The townsmen who for so long had despised him and thrown bottles in his corn now urged him to buckle down to the job of feeding them, and meanwhile sent him their children to look after.

Politicians uttered some ringing new promises to replace those they had broken. They offered him shepherdesses instead of shepherds, and hoped he would have no conscientious objection to employing conscientious objectors.

From time to time he would be overrun by troops, some of whom had been taught by the War Office to distinguish between grassland and young crops, and some not.

Affable gentlemen calling themselves war agricultural committees tramped over his fields, then sat down in his kitchen and told him what to grow. In Whitehall, anonymous gentlemen issued orders which forbade him, among other things, to kill a pig, to supply potatoes directly to a fish supper shop, to move loads of hay at night, and to load beet lorries in such a way that the beet fell off on the highway. They also informed him that summer would start in February." [2]

In spite of all food production efforts, new restrictions were imposed in July on food supplies. Hotels and restaurants were forbidden to serve both a fish and a meat course in the same meal. Icing on confectionary was forbidden — which meant the end of the traditional wedding cake. Meatless pies and strangely labelled tinned fish began to appear. From July 9th tea was rationed to two ounces per person per week. In Norfolk, Bunty Carr noted "everyone going around the village shops trying to get some extra tea". A couple of weeks later a combined ration of six ounces of butter and margarine, plus two ounces of cooking fat, per person per week was instituted. Soon afterwards everyone was busy making jam, urged on by the Women's Institutes, which set up bottling centres.

These stalwart efforts in the countryside were matched in the factories. There were not many armaments factories in East Anglia, but those there were set a cracking pace. Garretts, situated near a vulnerable stretch of coast at Leiston, at first made plans to evacuate to the Midlands, but then armed itself to the teeth instead, and carried on producing guns close to the beaches which might well have been the scene of invasion. The firm, with Admiralty consent but at its own expense, installed six 12-pounder guns at strategic points around the town. In a quiet country town like Beccles, one could have found a factory where women were making 20-pound mortar bombs. Boulton and Paul, in Norwich, was producing wooden fuselages for Oxford Trainer aircraft and nose sections for gliders and at Dereham, the Hobbies factory was changed from the manufacture of fretwork sets and other "practical" equipment for creative leisure to products capable of deadly destruction.

Schoolboys helping out in a Norfolk harvest field.   *Eastern Daily Press*

Members at Brooke, one of sixty Women's Institutes' Canning Centres which had been opened in Norfolk, dealing with the fruit brought in for preservation. *Eastern Daily Press*

Churchill brought the energetic propagandist-organiser Lord Beaverbrook into the government to boost defence production. "Women of Britain," cried his Lordship on July 5th, "give us your aluminium. We want it, and we want it now . . . We will turn your pots and pans into Spitfires and Hurricanes, Blenheims and Wellingtons . . ." Intense efforts were made to reprocess not only aluminium, but materials of every kind. There were organised collections of metals and of waste paper in every town and village. In Wisbech:

"The W.V.S. appealed to the housewives to hand over their aluminium pans, and the aluminium rolled in. A lot of it was serviceable and virtually irreplaceable perhaps for years. The whole was organised on the Market Place and, apart from the aluminium collection, there was an appeal for iron and waste paper. Started off by a cannon from the grammar school, relic of 1914-18, everything imaginable in iron came. There were old swords and huge iron wheels, and one man rode a bicycle up to the heap and threw it on." (3)

At Cambridge the decorative cast-iron railings around the colleges were cut down and handed over; many people donated their front gates; Colchester Town Council lost the last of its old tramway lines, three and a half miles of which were torn up from the High Street, Magdalen Street, Barrack Street and Hythe Hill. Southwold Town Council, in a burst of fervent patriotism, offered as scrap five of six old cannon which stood on Gun Hill. They were believed to be relics of the 1745 Rebellion, captured on the field of Culloden and presented to the town by the Duke of Cumberland. Protests came from near and far, and the Council rescinded its offer*.

Emmanuel College, following the lead of other foundations, disposed of their railings for war purposes.

Cambridge Evening News

The dogged efforts of the factory workers produced remarkable results. The R.A.F. had had only 700 front-line fighters in May, including 177 built in March and 256 in April. But the factories turned out 325 in May, 446 in June and 496 in July. Deliveries of other equipment was also stepped up spectacularly: tanks were produced at the rate of 123 a month during the summer and the delivery of field guns rose in consecutive months from 42 to 60 to 72.

And yet people were impatient, that summer, for more to be done. A Mass Observation report from Norwich stated:

"There is very little talk about the war in Norwich or the neighbouring Norfolk villages. People often get irritated if the general war situation is brought up in conversation.

*Much later, it was established that these guns could not have been used at Culloden and were, in fact, sent to Southwold in 1746 by the Master General of the Ordnance, on the instructions of the Privy Council. The facts are given in a booklet *The Southwold Guns*, by Major General P. J. Mackesy, published by the Southwold Archaeological and Natural History Society of 1965.

They seem fed up with the present lull and to be quite eager for the conflict to intensify itself. They are not interested in minor war news, which pales in dramatic value after the events in France.

British war bulletins seem to be believed by the majority and the R.A.F. is on a peak of popularity. Spontaneous clapping breaks out in cinemas when newsreels show air attacks beaten off." [4]

The cinema was still the most popular form of entertainment. Horse racing stopped after mid-June, but greyhound racing continued on one evening in each week. Occasionally a local cricket team played a scratch match against an Army team. The roads were almost completely deserted, except for military traffic. Most petrol pumps had been closed down. The newspapers now published regularly stamp-sized photographs of local men who had been killed or were posted missing. People dressed more soberly, perhaps on purely practical grounds. Many women had given up wearing stockings, and silk squares and scarves had become the most popular headwear. The rule when buying clothes was to look for "something sensible" that would last.

There was a heightened consciousness of danger. One in five now carried a gasmask (but almost everyone in the coastal areas), whereas it had been estimated during the previous April that not more than one in a thousand did so. The frequent air raids gave the A.R.P. services a great deal to do, and they reached a peak of efficiency. A Control Centre such as the one in Norwich was an impressive operation during an "incident". Those on duty included the Chief A.R.P. Officer, the Rest Centre Officer, liaison officers from the Police and the Fire Service, and representatives of the telephone, electricity, gas and water undertakings. When the threat of invasion seemed real, an officer of the Norwich Garrison stood by to plot any enemy landings. Warnings of possible raids reached the Control Centre from the R.A.F. and reports on local incidents came in over the direct lines from the Police Station, the Home Guard HQ and the National Fire Service HQ, or by telephone from the 82 wardens' posts, the first-aid posts, the ambulance depots, or the Rescue Party depots. All incidents were plotted on a very large map, and all were later reported to the Regional Commissioner's office in Cambridge.

Now that urban residential areas had come under attack, a network of "rest centres" had been brought to readiness to receive those whose homes had been destroyed but who had themselves survived. Most of these centres were in schools or church halls and they were manned by Women's Voluntary Service workers and schoolteachers. They were not merely shelters, but advisory centres where lost ration books and identity cards could be replaced, advice given on billeting and, if necessary, temporary financial assistance provided.

After the first air raid on Norwich there was strong feeling because the bombs had fallen before the warning siren was heard. Norwich Trades

Council called a delegate conference of all unions in the city and sent a warning to the Regional Commissioner that production would be disorganised unless the warning system was improved. A few days later the Clerk of the City Corporation issued a statement:

> "I am aware that there is considerable indignation in the city because the air raid sirens are not sounded . . . I have spoken personally to the Regional Commissioner, Sir Will Spens, on the telephone and asked him to make urgent representations."

The problem was that when single bombers ranged freely over large areas of the countryside, it was difficult for Fighter Command to decide when a warning should be sent to any particular neighbourhood. Three more raids on Norwich followed without sirens in advance of the bombs. Although it was only one plane each time, damage was considerable. On July 19th several homes and two shops were completely demolished and the premises of the Norwich Aero Club were burnt out, although there were no casualties. On July 30th ten people were killed or seriously injured when practically all the modest homes in Victoria Terrace were devastated and other bombs fell on the Surrey Street bus station, on Colman's printing shop at Carrow and opposite the old *Angel Hotel*. On August 1st six women and three men were killed when four bombs hit the paint shop at Boulton and Paul's Riverside Works, and several others were killed when the same plane machine-gunned the area around Thorpe station.

It was a difficult time, but the authorities could offer no encouragement. Back in June Winston Churchill had dictated a memorandum beginning: "Everyone should learn to take air raids and air raid alarms as if they were no more than thunderstorms . . ." [5] On July 2nd the government asked workers on war production to stay at their benches "until it is clear that an enemy attack is actually imminent in their neighbourhood". In mid-August Sir John Anderson announced that sirens would no longer be sounded for single aircraft. There was "a considerable shift from a policy of safety first to one of production first". [6] Workers at Colmans, Boulton and Paul and Laurence Scott agreed that they would work through the public "alerts" and rely solely on their own roof spotters. These firms created their own independent warning system and built their own spotting posts. This was the system that soon became almost universal.

The situation in the coastal regions was quite extraordinary. By September the population of the Clacton urban district was down from a prewar figure of 25,000 to something between 3,000 and 4,000. "Most business places have been closed down. Many traders have been ruined," reported the *Essex County Standard*. "The Urban Council carries on as best it can . . ." Several Fleet Street journalists visited the town, and one of them wrote:

"It is sad to drive along the deserted front. Here and there an empty car park, shops all boarded up, theatres closed, and restaurants deserted . . .

You can go down whole streets of boarded-up villas without meeting a soul. In some parts of the town you will find the military and, strangely enough, there are a few children . . ." [7]

At the *Royal Hotel*, however, Councillor Arthur Green, the manager, was determined to try to keep "Business as usual" and at one event in that dire opening week of September he had 300 people dancing in his ballroom.

Mass Observation sent two investigators into the "prohibited area" of Woodbridge-Aldeburgh at the end of August. Although they drove in by car, they went around in the district for 24 hours without being challenged! At Aldeburgh they found one hotel shut and the other completely abandoned, many of the shops boarded, tanks traps on the beach, and notices everywhere about the various orders concerning cars, curfew and access to the beach. In their report they observed:

"Considering that the town is now perhaps one of the quietest and dullest places in Britain, the degree of depression and irritation in Aldeburgh is not remarkably high. There are a great many local grievances, apparently largely due to the necessary restrictions imposed by the military and civil authorities. Extremely unpleasant things are said about local leaders, and numerous unfavourable (and probably often exaggerated) stories of local red tape are current . . .

Plenty of people have left the town and some have returned again. Those who have never left express frequent contempt for the others or show a feeling of superiority towards them . . ." [8]

In response to Lord Beaverbrook's appeal for aluminium, Mrs Sylvester, Leiston's organiser, is seen with the girder work of Zeppelin L48 which was brought down at Theberton 23 years earlier.

East Anglian Daily Times

This Mass Observation team also explored some of the surrounding villages and about these they reported:

"In the smaller villages of the area, Snape, Butley, Hollesley, Ramsholt, etc it would be possible to spend several hours in a village pub without realising that there was a war on . . . The position can best be summarised by saying that people are quite ready to say they don't like the war, but quite ready to stick it. There is a marked absence of any close emotional association with the war. Investigators noticed, on several occasions, distinct signs of a lack of friendliness towards the numerous soldiers in the area, and there was some antagonistic talk about them."

Their overall impression, however, was that morale in that region of Suffolk was appreciably higher than in London or the Midlands.

All the coastal towns were in similar plight. Lowestoft had lost at least half its normal population by July and half of its houses were empty. There were places where the exodus had been even greater: 70 per cent of the residents of Walton-on-the-Naze moved away, and in Southend 28,000 of its 50,000 houses were unoccupied after 90,000 out of a prewar population of 140,000 had evacuated. [9]

A local author described the situation in Lowestoft as "a life of continual apprehension — the raids so sudden that they were almost over before the noise of battle had begun. The roar of hostile planes unseen in low cloud, the thud of bombs, bursts of machine-gun fire, and it was all over . . ." [10] Apart from the danger, the war had changed all the daily routines of the town. Vast areas were closed to the public; the waterfront was entirely taken over by the defence services, and the place swarmed with sailors. There were pill-boxes and barricades at many strategic points and the whole district was surrounded by anti-tank defences, including miles of barbed wire. Posters were everywhere, spelling out the restrictions and encouraging evacuation.

But, in fact, from late summer people began to return to their homes. A barmaid in Lowestoft told Mass Observation: "People aren't frightened. All the people who left are coming back. A lot went from here to Norwich, thinking it was safer inland, but they've got it more than anywhere."

"The trainees returned to their boarding houses for lunch each day, so that four times each day the streets were full of masses of men leaving or converging on Sparrows Nest. The Germans noted this and their planes came in to machine-gun the men, who dived down flat. Basic training proceeded; square bashing at the Oval, a former sports ground on the seafront, quite close to the Sparrows Nest." [11]

For the local authorities, the consequences of mass evacuation were very serious. Their rate income dropped catastrophically. The problem had been

An armoured train near Saxmundham. It carried two 3-in. guns and a number of Bren guns: it was manned by 26 men.

Imperial War Museum

foreseen and representations were first made to the government during 1939. Deputations visited Whitehall early in 1940, and again in July, to put the case for the local authorities representing east and south-east coast boroughs. The Ministry of Health held rigidly to the attitude that authorities must take all other steps open to them to raise money — such as increasing the level of rates and arranging loans from their banks — before coming to the government for aid. Rate increases, the Ministry officials declared at the July meeting, had not yet moved "outside the normal range".

The Ministry ordered a survey of the position as it was at June 30th. Southend had overspent by £200,000, but was operating with a £36,000 overdraft and a £200,000 term loan from the bank. Great Yarmouth had an overdraft of £20,000 and had arranged a £50,000 bank loan. Southwold was reported to have "ample funds for two months if they don't pay the County Council precept". That was the solution which was already being adopted by the Clacton and Walton councils. Harwich had no overdraft and had arranged a £10,000 loan from the Crown Agents. Aldeburgh had exhausted its balances and had no reserve funds. [12]

None of this was sufficient to melt the hearts of the Ministry. They did take notice, however, when the Southwold Council suddenly announced that it had no option but to dismiss the whole of its staff! The Regional Commissioner quickly intervened to prevent that action. The whole problem of these coastal towns was referred to the War Cabinet at its meeting on August 2nd, when the Lord Privy Seal reported that Lowestoft was "in the hands of a bank", which, indeed, was the position of several of the authorities. The Chancellor of the Exchequer was unrelenting. War expenditure at this time was running at the rate of nine million pounds a day. If and when the government felt it must offer aid to the east coast towns, the Chancellor said, "there should be no attempt to reach a final settlement during the war"; by which he meant that the possibility should be left open that such aid would be in the form of loans, repayable when the war was over.

In fact, there was no government aid during 1940, and the controversy rumbled on. Great Yarmouth Council estimated that its deficit for the year ended March 1941 would be £84,000 and it instructed the town clerk to seek an advance of this sum from the Ministry. The Ministry, however, ordered another review of the whole problem, as at October 31st, and this suggested that Great Yarmouth actually had a surplus of £3,600 at that date. What was undeniable was that only just over half of the rates due from the previous year had actually been collected.

Life on the home front was full of problems to which there were no evident solutions. There was, nonetheless, a dogged determination to put the best possible face upon the situation. In many windows patriotic texts were prominently displayed. One of the most ubiquitous in that long, grim summer read: "We are not interested in the possibilities of defeat — they do not exist".

CHAPTER NINE

The Long Haul

A S AUTUMN set in and hardened into winter, the war in the air changed in character. Now the East Anglians saw fewer fighter planes darting and weaving in day-time combat. Instead their nights were disturbed by the deep throbbing of laden bombers "passing overhead like one long rumbling train". [1]

R.A.F. Bomber Command bases in the region now despatched their squadrons to attack targets all over the Continent, and, as they flew eastwards, the Luftwaffe formations carried *their* bombs to London and the major industrial cities of Britain.

The first bombs on residential districts of London were probably intended for industrial targets in the Thames estuary, but the attack called forth an immediate R.A.F. reprisal raid on Berlin on August 25th/26th, followed by others on succeeding nights. On September 4th Hitler promised the Berliners should have revenge, and three days later the Luftwaffe attack was switched from the R.A.F. Fighter Command stations to targets in London.

Just as in the Spring Britain had had barely adequate defences to ward off the daylight attacks, now in the autumn the night-time assaults stretched resources to the limit. In September, of the sixty R.A.F. fighter squadrons, only eight and a half were specialists in night fighting. [2] For many months great efforts had been made to equip the R.A.F. with air-to-air radar, so that fighter pilots might find their quarry in the darkness. On July 23rd a Blenheim had actually shot down a German bomber with the aid of airborne radar for the first time; but the Blenheim was not a suitable plane for the new night operational role. The first generation of aircraft specifically designed to combat night raiders, the Bristol Beaufighter, was not delivered to the R.A.F. until August and was not operational until the last few months of the year. Some of the first of them arrived at Debden in October, to join No 25 Squadron, but this was still a mixed squadron, with some Blenheims, as the year ended. The development of night fighter strength and skill was given top priority. No 85 Squadron at Debden and No 73 Squadron at Castle Camps, both flying Hurricanes, were designated for night operations at this time.

The defence activities of the night fighter squadrons were coordinated with those of the anti-aircraft gun-sites. These weapons, too, were in short supply — only 1,311 in the whole of Britain in September. [3] In the late summer, the number of them in East Anglia had had to be reduced in order to

The British Blenheim IV was the main stay of the light bomber force operating from aerodromes in East Anglia during 1940.   *Kinsey*

reinforce the south-eastern defences. Harwich had seventeen heavy A.A. guns in July, but the number was down to eight by early September. Ipswich had four in July, but only two after the end of August. Norwich, on the other hand, did not get heavy A.A. guns until the end of August, when four arrived around the city. The numbers allocated to the aerodromes in the region remained constant: four each at Martlesham and Wattisham, near the coast, and two each at the stations inland, Duxford, Feltwell, Marham, Watton and Horsham St Faith.

Many of the enemy air fleets crossed the coast of East Anglia on their way to their industrial targets inland, and so these defences were kept fully stretched. After the blitz on London had eased, the mass attacks began on Coventry, Birmingham, Liverpool and Sheffield. When the first raid took place on Coventry, wave after wave of German bombers arrived over East Anglia until the skies were full of the largest concentration of planes ever known there. Bunty Carr lay in bed in her North Norfolk village, listening to the roar of aircraft engines and of A.A. gunfire, and pondered:

"Planes going over all night from 9 p.m. Hundreds must have gone through. I wonder as I lie and hear the hum and the wallops in the distance where they are going, for somewhere is going to get a trouncing.

I also wonder how the pilots feel. After all, somebody loves them, even if they are Nazis, and they are risking their lives and fighting for their country, the same as our men that go bombing. How long can it go on?"

Trevor Bevis, living a little further west, heard and saw more:

"I remember well the town of March being rudely awakened in the small hours as the first droves of straining aircraft carried thousands of bombs to ill-fated Coventry. Half an hour later the final wave of planes could be heard droning in a westerly direction. Three quarters of an hour after

134

the first wave of bombers had passed, March residents heard distant explosions, missiles raining upon Coventry, nearly 80 miles away. Most people left their beds and took to the streets to watch the western sky turn from blackness to glowing orange. Then, about 35 minutes later, the sound of racing aero engines filled the sky above March as the German planes sped home." [4]

While most of the deadly cargoes passed harmlessly over the towns and villages of the eastern counties, they suffered their own tribulations. There was scarcely a day when the sirens were not wailing somewhere, and on most nights, too. The coastal areas continued to receive the constant attention of hit-and-run raiders, and single planes apparently flying without specific objectives began to harass inland areas to a much greater extent than during the summer months. Chelmsford, for example, did not hear a siren until June, when there were seven alerts, followed by a raid-free July; but then followed 27 alerts during August, 79 during September, and ninety during each of October and November, falling back to 35 during December. In one of the October raids a single plane dropped a bomb which demolished the home of the Mayor of Chelmsford, Alderman J. O. Thompson, killing the Mayor and Mayoress, three other members of their family, and a maidservant. It was in October, too, that 289 bombs fell in a single day on Norfolk—the greatest number on the county in any one day throughout the war. One hundred of them were aimed at West Raynham aerodrome. On the following day, October 28th, a total of 217 bombs on Norfolk was logged.

The western side of the region also now received regular attention from the Germans. Wisbech was bombed several times, and Chatteris and several of the villages in the area were attacked at different times. One of the obvious targets in this area, the vast railway marshalling yards at Whitemoor, was never effectively bombed, however, though one or two of the raids may have been aiming for it. A decoy yard was created about two miles away from the real target, using oil drums and shaded lights.

New hazards appeared. One took the form of "land mines" dropped by parachute. These drifted down without warning from the night skies and caused great devastation. Sometimes they failed to explode, and then experts were called in to perform the delicate and highly dangerous task of defusing

The 1 Kg. German Incendiary Bomb was 2-in. in diameter and 13½-in. in length.
Eastern Daily Press

135

them. These "bomb disposal squads" also dealt with high explosive bombs which failed to detonate, and sometimes there were tragic consequences. At Worlingworth, in East Suffolk, a bomb dropped on September 23rd blew up on October 10th while efforts were being made to defuse it, and five soldiers and a policeman were killed.

From mid-October the Germans mixed incendiaries with their high explosive bombs, and this called for a major reorganisation of the air raids precautions services. A new National Fire Service was established, in place of the local brigades, and it was supplemented by a civilian Fire Guard. This new organisation of "fire-watchers" began on a voluntary basis, but was quickly made compulsory for all adults. The possibility of heavy raids with incendiary bombs had long been foreseen. A leaflet distributed before the war began had stated:

> "It is probable that an enemy would make use of fire bombs . . . In every house there should be one or more people ready to tackle a fire bomb . . . If you have no stirrup handpump available, sand could be used to cover the bomb. This will not extinguish it, but you should be able to scoop up the remains of the bomb, drop them into a bucket containing about four inches of sand, and remove the bucket to a safe place." [5]

Unfortunately, stirrup pumps were still in short supply. Householders were asked to keep a bucket full of water standing outside their homes to serve as an emergency supply, and the A.R.P. services were given intensive training. It was at this time that the initials A.R.P. were replaced by a new designation of Civil Defence Services.

The autumn brought a reminder that the Germans were not the only enemy. On October 25th, for the first time, the Italian air force attacked Britain. Sixteen Fiat bombers took off from an airfield in Belgium; one of them crashed almost immediately, and the other fifteen made for Harwich. The small number of bombs which were dropped near the town suggested that only half of the planes arrived over the target. During the return flight, two of the Italian planes ran out of fuel and the crews baled out. There was another Italian attack on November 5th, when eight bombers bombed Harwich.

On November 11th the Italians made their only major daylight attack on Britain of the whole war. Ten bombers made for Harwich, accompanied by forty biplane fighters. The British radar stations reported at 1.30 p.m. that a heavy enemy force was approaching the Essex coast and thirty Hurricanes scrambled from Martlesham and North Weald and intercepted off the coast. There is disagreement about what followed. R.A.F. Fighter Command pilots claimed six bombers and three fighters destroyed, without loss. The Italians claimed nine British fighters destroyed; certainly, some are known to have been damaged in forced landings. What is beyond question is that the raiders were successfully deflected from their target and that four of their planes came down on British soil. One of the bombers crashed at Woodbridge and another at Bromeswell. One of the fighters ended up on the beach at Orford, and another flew very low along the main street of Lowestoft and landed in a field at Corton. When farm workers approached, the pilot enquired: "Is this Deutschland?"

At the end of November the Italians claimed to have bombed Ipswich, but, in fact, it was over Lowestoft and Great Yarmouth that nine of their bombers appeared, in the early evening. Six bombs hit the Co-operative Wholesale Society's canning factory in Waveney Drive, Lowestoft, extensively damaging the building, machinery and stocks of preserved foods, and killing three men.

There was a good deal of machine-gunning of streets and railways during the autumn and winter. A particularly sadistic pilot must have been at work on Sunday, November 3rd, for reports came in from all over East Anglia of buses, cars and pedestrians attacked by planes which roared low over housetops. In one such attack, at Somerleyton, the railway station and the

A Fiat BR 20 twin-engined bomber which was shot down among the young conifers in Tangham Forest, Woodbridge by Hurricanes from Martlesham Heath.   *Kinsey*

Duke's Head inn were singled out for attack. In another, at Bury St Edmunds, bullets sprayed the area around the railway station and the *Spread Eagle* inn. A month later, on December 4th, a bomber tried to hit a train travelling between Burwell and Fordham, in Cambridgeshire. Eighteen high explosive bombs straddled the track, tore up fifty yards of it, and blasted the roofs off some of the carriages. The plane then dived and machine-gunned the length of the train; two R.A.F. men who looked out of a carriage window were wounded. There was a similar attack on another train elsewhere in the region just before Christmas. The German plane dived and made nine consecutive runs at this train, shooting it up from about 70 yards range. The train crew and some of the passengers leapt down to the track and dived into a ditch, but the fireman was injured by a bullet.

As an odd contrast to these murderous attacks, the Germans dropped propaganda leaflets in East Anglia suggesting that the arming of the Home Guard had broken the accepted rules of war. These leaflets carried a photograph of Winston Churchill, holding a tommy-gun, captioned: "Wanted for Incitement to Murder". On the other side was the message:

> "This gangster who you see in his element in the picture incites by his example to participate in a form of warfare in which women, children and ordinary citizens shall take a leading part. This absolutely criminal form of warfare WHICH IS FORBIDDEN by the Hague Convention will be punished according to military law. Save at least your families from the horrors of war."

Naturally, this message was not well received, for by this time a lot of "women, children and ordinary citizens" had been killed. One small hospital and a home for elderly evacuated women had been bombed and some patients had been killed; the almshouses at Framlingham had been extensively damaged by bombs; the 15th century church at Little Horkesley had been levelled to the ground, and the tower of the church of St Peter ad Vincula at Coggeshall had been wrecked; and other buildings which had been more or less destroyed included the Roman Catholic church at Aldeburgh, the Constitutional Club at Southwold, and several schools. No country town was too remote and no village too small to be picked out for attention.

The larger towns continued to bear the brunt of the attack, particularly those along the coast, which were visited by the Luftwaffe quite regularly. Norwich was raided six times during the period of the Battle of Britain, and then suffered seven more attacks before the year ended. A raid in September caused more inconvenience than damage; a 1,000-lbs delayed-action bomb buried itself in the street just outside the Theatre Royal, where the Arts Ballet Company was performing. For nearly a week the whole area had to be evacuated. Just after teatime on Sunday, October 27th four raiders roared over at only about 100 feet and began by spraying streets with machine-gun bullets. They then dropped several strings of bombs, which damaged the Norwich Aero Club hangar and a number of houses in Mousehold, Thorpe and St Faiths, but no-one was killed. During November there were two raids by single planes, which dropped incendiary bombs which did little harm.

There was naturally acute concern about the danger to Norwich's historic buildings, and the worst was feared when, through a damp winter fog during the early evening of December 2nd, bombs were heard whistling down in the immediate area of the cathedral. One fell in the Cloisters and cracked some buttresses and blasted some leaded windows to a height of 60 feet. Another fell in the area between the north transept and the Bishop's Palace, but it failed to explode. It disappeared down a disused well. A squad of Royal Engineers tried to dig it out of the soft, sandy soil at the bottom, but it sank into water, and they had to give up the task. After that, prayer was the appropriate remedy. Other bombs dropped during that raid left families buried deep beneath the wreckage of their homes in St Johns Street, and when the Rescue Parties dug them out, four were dead and two others seriously injured. The centre of Morgan's Brewery was demolished by another bomb, and beer ran out in a great river. A lorry-driver from Wymondham driving along Riverside saw a bomb open up a large crater in front of him; his lorry dived into it, but he escaped.

Stories of "miraculous" escapes and of the freak effects of explosions were, of course, commonplace at this time. When a lone raider dropped several bombs on Norwich on December 11th, one hit a small terraced house in

Carrow Vale. An 83-year-old pensioner was blasted from his bedroom and deposited in his front garden, unhurt and still tucked up in bed. He had refused to take shelter downstairs; his 18-year-old grand-daughter, who had done so, was killed.

There was an unfortunate episode a few days later when a British plane released bombs over Norwich and one hit a garage in Bond Street. By the time the year ended, the city had had 580 alerts, totalling well over 640 hours, and sixty of its citizens had been killed and 190 injured.

The other principal towns of East Anglia did not suffer as badly. Ipswich, in the period between the end of the Battle of Britain and the year-end, was bombed nine times. The only deaths, however, occurred in a raid on October 27th, when seven men were killed in the port area, and another raid on November 4th, when a boy was killed in Bloomfield Street. Incendiary bombs were scattered over a wide area during the night of November 10th, some landing on the Catholic Hall, on the greyhound stadium, on three different schools, and on a laundry. In the town's last raid of the year, on December 21st, a mixture of incendiaries and high explosives hit the borough general hospital and a school.

Colchester and Cambridge were also attacked again. Three girls were killed when bombs wrecked a Colchester laundry on October 3rd, and one person was killed when a single bomb fell on Cambridge on October 15th. The Germans also continued to attack R.A.F. stations from time to time; on Sunday, October 27th, for example, they blasted Coltishall, Feltwell and Martlesham.

Most people began to get accustomed to the raids, and were less inclined to allow them to interfere with normal activities. Bunty Carr noted in her diary:

"Many planes and bombs heard during the night. But this morning hardly anybody seems to have heard it and no-one seems particularly interested in where the bombs fell. They have got used to idea and as long as they're not hit themselves, they don't bother, like they did at first."

Apart from falling bombs, falling aeroplanes were a constant hazard. There could have been few people who did not watch one come down at one time or another. Often crews baled out, floated down on parachutes, and were prompty taken into custody by Home Guard or police. In one remarkable incident, on October 20th, a German crew baled out of a Dornier bomber over Salisbury Plain, but the aircraft flew on for 120 miles towards its base before making a gentle belly-landing on the foreshore at Shotley, Essex. Almost as strange was the arrival on the runway of Oakington aerodrome on September 19th of a Junkers 88a carrying valuable photographic equipment—just two months before the R.A.F. formed a photographic reconnaissance unit at this same base.

A captured German Dornier 17 on exhibition at Eaton Park, Norwich during September.

Eastern Daily Press

German planes which were brought down in one piece were trucked around from town to town and exhibited in public parks and other open spaces — a Dornier was exhibited during October, for example, on Crown Meadow at Lowestoft. These displays were part of a campaign to increase war savings in so-called "Spitfire Funds". It was obviously important to damp down consumer demand for goods, and the public was encouraged to put every spare penny into savings. The people of Norwich set a record in 1940 by saving £27 a head: a total of £3,386,926.

Apart from the official campaign, individuals rallied support. When a high explosive bomb fell at the rear of the *Saracen's Head Hotel* in Chelmsford, the manager roped off the area and charged one shilling to inspect the crater; this raised over £100 towards the cost of a new fighter plane.

There were many souvenir hunters, searching the ground, after any battle overhead, for cartridge cases and pieces of planes. At Reach, by the Devil's Ditch in Cambridgeshire, there was an incendiary raid on October 5th, but only three of the missiles landed on houses and all fires were extinguished within thirty minutes. The children from the village school then went out searching and their teacher recorded their finds; between them, they collected 213 tail fins from the bombs.

R.A.F. Bomber Command maintained its offensive throughout these months, with the East Anglian bases fully engaged. From September, a Czech bomber squadron based at Honington flew Wellingtons to many parts of Europe, including Berlin. Another squadron based there bombed the industrial area around Venice during December. Squadrons from Feltwell, West Raynham, Marham and Wretham took part in regular raids on factories, oil plants, airfields, ports and communications in Germany; one of the most frequently-attacked targets was the railway marshalling yard at Hamm.

Once the danger of invasion appeared to have passed, the disposition of Army units was again changed significantly. It was recognised, even as winter set in, that landings from enemy transports *might* still be possible in small harbours and on beaches anywhere between Orfordness and Poole, and two field divisions remained in Kent and one in Norfolk. All other troops, however, were withdrawn from defensive postures for intensive training. [6] By November seven county divisions, each with 10,000 men (but with very little artillery or transport), were undergoing courses of mobile warfare. Most of these men had a tough time and, before the winter was over, they had become used to the idea of going into action immediately after completing a forced march of forty miles on foot. They had rehearsed the hypothetical battles of 1941 over and over again. The idea of a counter-invasion campaign was still uppermost in the military mind, and there was much practice in rounding up parachutists and careful planning of special routes for the movement of military traffic and for smooth flow of refugees. [7]

Members of the East Suffolk Youth Service formed an efficient children's fire brigade.

East Anglian Daily Times

The plan prepared for the Norwich area designated a number of "military roads to be kept clear of all civilian traffic", and other "roads to be used for civilian evacuees". There were five separate "refugee routes" by which those driven from their homes might be directed across the city and out into the open country to the west. Two of them provided for entry by Thorpe Road and exit by Newmarket Road; the other three concentrated at Mile Cross Road and then divided into two streams, to leave either by Earlham Green Lane or Christchurch Road. Military police were to be posted at a large number of designated control points. The military plan for Norwich concluded: "All private cars to be immobilised immediately. Cars still on the roads will be immobilised by the Military Authorities. Information concerning parachutists will be given to (1) Britannia Barracks, (2) R.A.F. St Faiths, (3) Air Ministry, Stoke, and (4) Regional Police Staff Officer."

The Home Guard was, by this time, considered to be sufficiently trained and equipped to take over many of the coastal defence duties. The 18th (East Anglian) Division, which had stood guard in Norfolk throughout all the stresses of the year (and which included the 4th Battalion of the Royal Norfolks and the 5th Battalion of the Suffolks, the pre-war Territorials), was among those withdrawn for training. The 5th Suffolks trained in the Cambridge area for about two and a half months. Nearby, at St Neots, the 4th Suffolks were similarly engaged. Some of the newer battalions moved into the coastal areas, alongside the Home Guard; the recently-formed 8th Battalion of the Suffolks, for example, was moved to Walton-on-the Naze and Frinton during October and given responsibility for four miles of coast. Its four companies were posted forward on the beaches and they spent the rest of the year erecting steel scaffolding and other defence works. There was a battery of medium guns behind them, but otherwise no attempt at defence in depth in that sector. [8]

Winston Churchill maintained a relentless pressure on his Army chiefs. Even after all these changes had taken place, he was still protesting in December that too many soldiers were not on combatant duty, but constituted what he termed "fluff and flummery behind the fighting troops". [9] As part of the general reorganisation at this time, Eastern Command was reduced in size by the creation of a new South-Eastern Command to take over all responsibilities south of the Thames.

The ports of East Anglia were now better armed. By November fixed artillery defences included four 6-inch and two 12-pounder guns at Great Yarmouth, the same strength at Lowestoft, two 9.2-inch, six 6-inch, two 12-pounder and three 6-pounder guns at Harwich, two 6-inch guns at King's Lynn, and two 4.7-inch guns at East Mersea.

The Germans maintained their effort in the North Sea without respite. From August they laid acoustic mines off the east coast and they began to fit delay devices to magnetic mines. Every night when the weather permitted they sent over seventy to eighty planes to lay these mines. The Royal Navy minesweepers, which by August were just beginning to maintain swept channels at all times, began to operate increasingly by night after August, in order to avoid air attack. By the end of September the important Would Channel, off Cromer, was reopened for the first time since December, 1939, and this enabled convoys to be routed closer inshore, where they could be assured of better fighter protection. [10]

Resources were tightly stretched. Bombing of the convoys continued, and from September E-boats began to appear to attack with torpedoes. Losses were heavy, among naval vessels as well as merchant ships. The Royal Naval Patrol Service lost more than 90 vessels between June and December, half of them blown up by mines, most of the others sunk by bombers. In November alone, 26 trawlers and drifters were lost. In September the Admiralty, facing the new menace of acoustic mines, sought to get some of the Auxiliary Patrol trawlers converted into minesweepers; at about the same time, the Ministries of Food and of Agriculture and Fisheries were urging that trawlers and drifters should be released to resume fishing. Eventually new measures were devised to deal with the acoustic mines, but these were not in use before the end of November, and they were far from perfect.

As during the early days of the war, Britain's seamen were now bearing the brunt of battle. The Germans were aiming, not only to destroy the productive capacity of the munitions factories by their night-time bombing raids, but simultaneously to starve out the British by a tighter blockade of the ports.

Anthony Eden, the War Minister, inspecting a support group of the 2nd Armoured Division near Whittlesford, Cambridgeshire, in September. *Imperial War Museum*

King George VI inspects a parade of officers and men from minesweepers at Gorleston in August.

Imperial War Museum

Perhaps it was a symbol of defiance that the official meat ration was increased from 1s.10d. to 2s.2d. per person per week from October. Other foodstuffs were getting more difficult. The butter ration was reduced to two ounces, and some unrationed items, including cheese and treacle, were unobtainable in some areas. In the country, rabbits had become an important part of the diet, and on fine days people went blackberrying and mushrooming with a new sense of purpose. At the same time, they gathered fir cones to supplement their fuel supplies, for on a number of occasions electricity supplies had been interrupted without explanation.

Farmers were again subject to exhortation. "Every available piece of grass shall be ploughed up for harvesting next autumn," it was officially decreed. The Norfolk War Agricultural Executive Committee announced that 50,000 acres would be ploughed for the 1941 harvest—an increase of 18,000 acres. The Ministry of Agriculture issued instructions that Norfolk must increase its potato crop by 3,000 acres, its onions by 700 acres, its dried peas by 1,250 acres, its haricot beans by 350 acres, its tomatoes under glass by eight acres, and its tomatoes out of doors by forty acres. Each county was given its set quotas in this way.

A big programme of mole draining had been completed in East Anglia, so that many more acres were available for cultivation. Work was now put in hand on major new drainage schemes, such as that to drain and provide roads for 6,000 acres of Feltwell Fen, in West Norfolk, at a cost of £50,000. A considerable stretch of Holkham Marshes was marked out for ploughing.

145

The countryside was invaded by a new wave of evacuees from London when the blitz began there. The task of billetting them was now more difficult because the Army had requisitioned almost all large houses, village halls and empty buildings of all kinds, and many private homes had soldiers billetted upon them, usually in pairs. Bunty Carr's diary notes:

William Gardiner from Stow-market Area School proudly discloses the success of the school National Savings week.

East Anglian Daily Times

"Evacuation meeting. Everyone is worried nearly to death in case they should get people billetted on them. No enthusiasm about them at all this year, like there was before. Everyone's seen them since then!"

In fact, many of the Londoners who turned up in East Anglia went home again within a few days, complaining that there were no shelters or alternatively that it was too quiet for them.

London's undergraduate evacuees returned to Cambridge for a new term and, outwardly at least, the life of the university was very much as usual. A total of 6,424 came up in October, including 1,706 evacuees: 537 from Bedford College, 458 from the London School of Economics, 261 from Queen Mary's College, 200 from Barts, 79 from the London Hospital, and 64 from the Bartlett School of Architecture. The restrictions imposed, on the eve of Dunkirk, on the debates of the Union Society were now re-examined. It was agreed that debates of a non-political character should be resumed "subject to certain restrictions", which were not published.

An undergraduate whose home was on Merseyside noted in his diary his preoccupations as he prepared to return to Cambridge:

"Have been thinking about this next Cambridge term: whether I can get any work done, if I drop rowing — a thing the other members of the Boat Club would regard as treachery in these days of depleted membership. What sort of air raids are we going to have; if there are as many per night as in Wallasey I'll be desperate, because our shelters are in the boiler room, and the atmosphere gets intolerable after half an hour. Then, most important, what will the music be like — will I be able to create a string quartet?" [11]

Efforts were maintained elsewhere to keep alive the arts and live entertainment. Colchester Repertory Company, after its summer tour of garrison theatres, was again performing regularly in the town. The Norwich Players had successfully kept the Maddermarket Theatre in business, rounding off their year with a production of *Twelfth Night* in modern fancy dress. The London Philharmonic Orchestra gave two concerns in Norwich in December. In a different genre, Tommy Handley and Jack Train, the stars of the popular ITMA radio show, performed at the Norwich Hippodrome during the week before Christmas.

Occasionally there were news items in the papers that had nothing to do with the war. A new Bishop of St Edmundsbury and Ipswich, the Venerable Richard Brook, was consecrated in the cathedral church at Bury St Edmunds on November 1st by the Archbishop of Canterbury. It was a unique occasion, inasmuch as all previous consecrations of bishops of the southern province had taken place in London. Bury witnessed its most impressive turn-out of bishops in modern history.

More sombre headlines resulted from a great fire in Norwich on the night of October 22nd/23rd. A score of shops and other premises in the business centre of the city, the area known as "Back of the Inns", were almost completely destroyed, but there was no loss of life. The *Castle Hotel* had to be evacuated, and was badly damaged. The whole area at the rear of the hotel and across to the Arcade (where three shops were burnt out) was affected, extending to the Haymarket public house and to the old Fifty Shilling Tailors' shop, which was destroyed. Amid a jungle of hoses, 200 firemen and police worked for hours to get the situation under control.

There was another serious fire on December 21st, at Long Melford, when the historic *Bull Hotel* was badly damaged.

Soon after the big Norwich blaze, twenty Norwich firemen volunteered to go to London to fight the blitz, changing places for a week with twenty London firemen. The visitors to Norwich were feted, staying as guests at the *Royal Hotel*. The Norwich men who went to London did not get their clothes off during the whole week.

In this and other ways it was brought home to people that East Anglia was suffering but minor inconvenience compared to the hardships endured elsewhere. The sirens continued to wail regularly. The anti-aircraft guns blasted away most nights — earplugs were distributed in Norwich during October to those who asked for them. The weather deteriorated and the blackout came down again like a pall. Motorists were prosecuted and fined because, according to one report, the sidelights on the cars "did not conform to recent emergency restriction regulations, that the light is emitted through a single circular aperture of one-inch diameter". Train services were sometimes dislocated. When the Carr sisters travelled by train from Hunstanton to Stowmarket, they were turned out at King's Lynn because there was a time bomb somewhere on the line. A bus was provided instead. One woman passenger arriving late on the scene hesitated to board it and the guard called out: "Get in, madam, this *is* the London train." Chuckles all round.

Volunteers from the Norwich A.F.S. setting out for London to relieve the hard-pressed London fire-men.
Eastern Daily Press

There were still restrictions on travel in the coastal belt, but from October the authorities began to discuss the possibility of relaxing the Defence Area restrictions imposed during the summer. The military and the civilian authorities took different views. The Army was firmly opposed to any public announcement of a relaxation, but agreed that local authorities might advise

148

their inhabitants quietly that it was permissible to return. On October 27th General Massy visited Sir Will Spens at Cambridge and strongly pressed his view, which prevailed for some weeks. In December, however, the Defence Area was reduced to a five-miles-wide coastal strip, and Ipswich and Colchester were excluded from it. As the year ended, the military were complaining that there had been too much slackening of control. The Commander of the 42nd Division made a formal complaint in December that anyone with a fishing rod was permitted on to the pier at Felixstowe, from which many of the defence works could be closely studied.

The military authorities had their reasons, although these could not be known elsewhere. Although the spy mania of the summer months had died down, the fact was that spies were now being parachuted into Britain, and several of them had made their way to East Anglia.

During the night of September 30th two men and a woman landed in a rubber dinghy on the coast of Banffshire, after having been flown there from Norway by seaplane. When they were arrested, only a few hours later, one of the men was found with a list of bomber and fighter stations in the eastern counties.

Early in September, two spies had arrived by parachute. For some time before leaving Germany, they had been together in a Hamburg hotel, where they were briefed and kitted out with English clothes, false papers, £200 each of unused pound notes, suitcase radio transmitters, and Luger revolvers. The first to arrive in Britain was a young Finn, Goesta Caroli, who came down by parachute north of Oxford during the night of September 6th. He was arrested almost immediately, interviewed at length by MI5 at their establishment at Richmond, Surrey, and successfully "turned round", that is, persuaded to work for the British. He was taken to Hinxton, just south of Cambridge and within a few miles of Duxford aerodrome, established there by the British authorities and directed to transmit misleading information to Germany.

When the second spy, Wulf Dietrich Schmidt, a Dane, arrived on September 19th, Caroli had been able to warn the British that he was coming. Schmidt was flown over in a Heinkel by the same pilot who had ferried in Caroli, but this time the drop was in Cambridgeshire. It did not go well for the spy. As he jumped, his metal wristwatch strap caught on something; the watch was damaged and blood began to spurt from a wrist injury. Schmidt landed on a road, winded, and sprained an ankle, and, to make matters worse for him, his parachute was caught up on telephone wires. He tore it down and hid it and when morning came he wandered into the nearest village. "I went into a shop to buy a watch," he recalled later. (12) "The woman started filling out a form and I thought: 'Cripes, you need a permit to buy a watch'. Then she stamped it. It was the guarantee. And the stamp gave the name of the shop and the village—Willingham." That was the village, just north of Cambridge where the police picked him up a few hours later.*

At least one other spy worked in the Cambridge area during 1940. He was a 27-years-old Dutchman, Jan Willen Ter Braak, who was dropped by parachute at Amersham, Bucks, on October 3rd, 1940. As well as the customary suitcase transmitter, currency and gun, he carried Red Cross letters addressed to refugees living in England, which had been intercepted by the German Secret Service; these were intended to provide him with a contact list. He made his way to Cambridge and took lodgings at three different addresses there: in Montague Road (interestingly, the road in which the Regional Commissioner's headquarters was accommodated), in Chesterton Road, and in St Barnabas Road. It seems that he, too, was quickly picked up by MI5 and it must be presumed that he was "turned round" by them. He was first noted in Cambridge early in November, when he was posing as a refugee and a member of the Free Dutch Movement, and stating that he was writing a book. He actually opened an office in Rose Crescent. Some of his activities attracted attention and more than one person reported on him to the local police. One man who regularly used a café on Peas Hill several times noticed that "a civilian, wearing a French-type beret, was always quizzing or conversing with R.A.F. service personnel". Both he and the café proprietor informed the police.† (13)

There were almost certainly other arrivals. On November 3rd, 1940, the Chief Constable's office at Ipswich circulated a memorandum it had received from the Buckinghamshire police, which read:

"Enemy parachute landing at 1200 hours 3rd November 1940. Complete enemy parachute, with harness, overalls and flying helmet, was found, neatly folded and placed under a hedge beside the bridle path at Holly Farm, near Amersham, Bucks. Parachute wet, but the clothing inside was dry, and it appears that it may have been dropped during the past two or three days . . . Parachute has, without doubt, been used and the parachutist landed uninjured and is still at large. There is no trace of crashed aircraft and the parachutist was without doubt deliberately dropped. Special enquiries and observation requested of military, Home Guard and police." (14)

*Schmidt worked for the British throughout the remainder of the war, and afterwards became naturalised, married, and settled in this country. In January 1981 he was reported to be living in Watford under a different name. Caroli worked for the British at Hinxton until, in January 1941, he attempted to escape. He was recaptured at Ely. In January 1941 the Germans were allowed to know that Caroli's radio transmitter had been deposited in the left luggage office at Cambridge railway station, and the German Secret Service then ordered another of their agents in England to collect it. This he did—but he, also, had been "turned round" to work for the British.

†Jan Willen Ter Braak was found shot dead in an air raid shelter on Christs Pieces in Cambridge on April 1st, 1941. It appears that he committed suicide, but at the time all mention of the matter was suppressed.

The Right Rev. Richard Brooks leaving the West Door of the Cathedral at Bury St Edmunds after being enthroned as Bishop of St Edmundsbury and Ipswich. *Eastern Daily Press*

Men from Norfolk and Suffolk, recently returned from the B.E.F., arrived in Sydney, Australia, in charge of German and Italian prisoners of war.

Eastern Daily Press

Not every spy was "turned round", for it was announced during December that three had been hanged in Pentonville Prison, in London — unless, of course, that was a false report issued to confuse the Germans further.

Of these special excitements, the public knew nothing.

Christmas now approached, in circumstances as unpropitious as one may imagine for a celebration of the season of goodwill. Already, during November, shops started displaying notices of what goods were NOT available, and by December the notices came down because everyone well knew what was unobtainable. Onions, lemons, eggs, slab chocolate, tinned milk and bananas were some of things which it was hardly worth enquiring about. Queues were now a regular feature of the shopping centres. In Bury St Edmunds John Allpress started early and worked hard to try to get together some Christmas fare, as his diary indicates:

November 16: I tried every fruit shop in the town for oranges, but no luck. Things beginning to get scarce and expensive.

November 19: After work, I cycled round the town to try to get some carrots; could not. Vegetables have become very scarce.

November 25th: After work, I cycled to Nices, the grocers, and was able to get two packets of Shredded Wheat and a jar of Rose's lime marmalade.

November 26th: Heard that no more bananas are to be imported. Bought some Lyons steamed puddings at Hoggs.

December 2nd: Milk supplies to be cut. No fruit (except oranges) to be imported.

December 3rd: Managed to buy some oranges.

152

A lorry arrived in Chelmsford market on December 20th with twelve cases of oranges and lemons and was brought under such a state of siege by women shoppers that the police had to intervene. The lorry retreated, the police restored order and marshalled a queue, and the fruit was then brought back to be sold.

Jenny Carr recorded on December 9th:

"Bunty has made our Christmas pudding today. We have been waiting a month for a hen to lay, to mix them up with, and yesterday she did it!"

Chickens sold at 9s.6d., which was very much more expensive than usual. There were fewer turkeys, and they were expensive, too. Something called "economy puddings" appeared in the shops. There were no Christmas trees in windows, no decorations in homes, and very few greetings cards. Some of the mail was delivered, for the first time since the first world war, by postwomen. Presents were chosen for their "usefulness", and were mostly knitted at home; there was no special decorative paper in which to wrap them. The Salvation Army bands turned out to play Christmas hymns, but there were none of the customary carol singers. Winston Churchill announced that church bells might be rung on Christmas Day. Jenny Carr's Christmas Day passed like this:

"Got up very late. Morning busy cooking the chicken and making mince pies. After lunch, we walked for milk and at about 3.30 p.m. went to our friends. Stayed until 10 p.m., having tea and supper (turkey), eating chocolates, one glass only of wine, playing cards, games and talking. Not too dull a time, considering party consisted of two widows, three old maids, and three young ones."

The traditional happy atmosphere was nowhere to be found that day. Norwich City arranged to play Brighton and Hove Albion at Carrow Road, and only 1,419 spectators turned up. Worse than that, their opponents turned up tired after an all-night journey by road, and one man short. A loudspeaker appeal was made to the crowd and a soldier came forward to complete the forward line. Norwich played with some of the Ipswich team in their line-up and won by eighteen goals nil, which was a Football League record and no satisfaction to anyone.

The brave pretence that something of the old traditions might be kept alive was maintained on Boxing Day, but with little more success. The Carr sisters attended the meet of the local hunt and reported that the riders included only women, children and men over fifty years of age. There were twenty carloads of sightseers, including some Servicemen and some Cockney school-children, and a party of Polish officers was invited to take sherry with the hunt.

Searchlights at the ready, to pick out hostile aircraft.

B.B.C. Hulton Picture Library

A Boxing Day ploughing match took place at Thurne, in Norfolk, as it had done for nearly a century, and a record 111 furrows were ploughed. The winner, Mr T. Dowe, ploughed a dead straight line for forty yards — "a plumb furrow" — which had only been achieved by two other competitors in the previous 28 years.

Christmas was soon over. The carting of sugar beet began again. The bombers came back. The newspapers published photographs of the bombed chamber of the House of Commons and accounts of a devastating raid which had set the City of London ablaze. The men and women of the Civil Defence services in East Anglia manned their posts and waited, and the firewatchers in every street scanned the night skies. And people fell to discussing the old familiar question: how long would this war continue? In the early part of 1940 there had been a widespread view that it would be a matter of months. Now the Prime Minister himself was talking about what might be achieved in 1943 and 1944. As people hunched their shoulders and thrust forward their heads, it was not the cold winter wind they braced themselves against, but the long haul ahead before they could hope to recreate the peace and the beauty of their East Anglian community.

The Duke of Gloucester, with staff officers, looks across the North Sea towards enemy territory during a tour of the East Coast in December. *Imperial War Museum*

Notes on Sources

Chapter 1

Most of the factual material in this chapter has been extracted from the files of the regional daily newspapers and most of the personal impressions and quoted opinions are drawn from personal diaries in the Mass Observation archive at Sussex University. As the observers and diarists who reported to Mass Observation during 1940 were promised confidentiality, it is necessary that I identify them by pseudonyms when quoting from their texts, but their words can be found in the archive exactly as I have printed them.

(1), (2), (3), (5) and (6) indicate the introduction of Mass Observation diarists whose real identity has been safeguarded in this way. (4) is an extract from the *Eastern Daily Press* of March 13th, 1940. (7) is an extract from a Mass Observation "Suffolk Village Report", No 170 in the archive.

Chapter 2

The basic text for factual information about A.R.P. and civil defence is Terence H. O'Brien's *Civil Defence*, one of the volumes in the official History of the Second World War, U.K. Civil Series. Another volume in this series, Richard M. Titmuss's *Problems of Social Policy* presents the facts about the various evacuation schemes.
(1) O'Brien, Page 185.
(2) O'Brien, Page 311.
(3) Public Record Office: Regional Commissioners' Registered Files (HO 207).
(4) O'Brien, Pages 176-7.
(5) O'Brien, Pages 346-50.
(6) O'Brien, Page 332.
(7) Titmuss, Page 172.
(8) Winston Churchill: *The Second World War*, Vol. 1, *The Gathering Storm*, Page 434.
(9) A. J. P. Taylor: *English History, 1914-1945*, Pages 461 and 515.

Chapter 3

The basic text for factual information about North Sea operations in 1940 is the first volume of Captain S. W. Roskill's *The War at Sea, 1939-45*. Details of specific attacks on shipping are from press reports at the time. Information about R.A.F. operations is given in detail in Michael J. F. Bowyer's *Action Stations — Wartime Military Airfields of East Anglia, 1939-45*. Information about Army dispositions in East Anglia is provided by the official history *The Defence of the United Kingdom*, by Basil Collier, and information about regiments in the British Expeditionary Force by the various regimental histories, but particularly Colonel W. N. Nicholson's *The Suffolk Regiment, 1928-46*. Mr Reg Dexter kindly provided his recollections for inclusion in this book.
(1) Roskill, Page 140.
(2) Roskill, Page 138.
(3) Report in *Eastern Daily Press*, January 13th, 1940.
(4) Churchill, Page 447.
(5) Bowyer.
(6) Denis Richards: *The Royal Air Force*, Vol. 1, *The Fight at Odds*.
(7) Nicholson.
(8) Collier.

Chapter 4

Information about the home front has been obtained from the regional daily newspapers and most of the impressions quoted come from the personal diaries in the Mass Observation archive. Information about the experiences of East Anglian Regiments in Belgium and France has been taken from the regimental histories, particularly Colonel Nicholson's *The Suffolk Regiment, 1928-46* and Tim Carew's *The Royal Norfolk Regiment.*

(1) *East Anglian Daily Times*, June 3rd, 1940.

(2) Titmuss, Page 190.

(3) "Suffolk Village Report", Mass Observation No 170.

(4) Ibid.

(5) O'Brien, Page 359.

(6) Mass Observation archive, personal diaries.

(7) Collier; also, Harry Hitchman: *Harwich, The Versatile Seaport.*

(8) Churchill, Pages 369-70.

(9) Churchill, Page 441.

(10) Col. T. A. Martin: *The Essex Regiment, 1929-50.*

(11) Nicholson, Page 56.

(12) Nicholson.

(13) Churchill, Page 52.

(14) Carew, Pages 113-4.

(15) *Eastern Daily Press*, June 14th, 1940.

(16) Hitchman; also, Paul Lund and Harry Ludlam: *Trawlers go to war*, Page 59.

(17) *East Anglian Daily Times*, December 31st, 1940.

(18) *Eastern Daily Press*, June 6th and 13th, 1940.

Chapter 5

(1) *Cambridge Review*, January 17th, 1941.

(2) "Suffolk Village Report", Mass Observation No 170.

(3) Peter Fleming: *Invasion 1940*, Page 24.

(4) Titmuss, Pages 242-3.

(5) *Eastern Daily Press*, March 29th, 1940.

(6) A. D. F. Gow: *Letters from Cambridge.*

(7) "Suffolk Village Report", Mass Observation No 170.

(8) Ibid.

(9) Roderick Macleod and Denis Kelly: *The Ironside Diaries*, Page 347.

(10) R. V. Jones: *Most Secret War*, Pages 114-8.

(11) O'Brien, Pages 632-3.

(12) R. J. Thompson: *Battle over Essex.*

(13) Collier, Page 105.

Chapter 6

One of the most important sources for the war in 1940 is *Their Finest Hour*, the second volume of Sir Winston Churchill's history, *The Second World War*. The basic text for factual information about the preparations for invasion is Basil Collier's *The Defence of the United Kingdom*. The first volumes of Captain S. W. Roskill's *The War at Sea* and Denis Richards' *The Royal Air Force* have the same importance in respect of the Royal Navy and the Royal Air Force. Michael J. F. Bowyer's *Action Stations—Wartime Military Airfields of East Anglia* contains much detailed information about this region. Charles Graves' *The Home Guard of Britain* gives the fullest account of the raising of this force, but the privately-published booklet *We Also Served, 1940-43* prepared by the Cambridgeshire and Isle of Ely Territorial Army

Association has been a more important source of information for this chapter. David Lampe's *The Last Ditch* offers the only comprehensive account of the Auxiliary Units. Information about Regional Commissioners' responsibilities and activities is provided by Terence H. O'Brien in *Civil Defence*, but most of the information in this chapter comes from the Regional Commissioners' Registered Files (HO 207) in the Public Record Office. Details of air raids have been obtained from local newspapers, from Joan Banger's *Norwich at War* and from an "Account of air raid attacks on Ipswich, 1940" prepared by a one-time Town Clerk, A. Moffat, and held by the Suffolk Record Office at Ipswich (HD 862).

(1) Collier, Page 124.
(2) Fleming, Page 185.
(3) *We Also Served*, Page 51.
(4) Ibid, Page 77.
(5) Ibid, Page 39.
(6) Fleming, Page 153.
(7) Churchill, Page 252.
(8) Collier, Page 129.
(9) Collier, Page 105.
(10) Collier, Page 105.
(11) Collier, Pages 124-5.
(12) Churchill, Page 151.
(13) Collier, Page 142.
(14) "Morale in Coastal Suffolk", Mass Observation Report No 372.
(15) *We Also Served,* Page 78.
(16) Churchill, Page 254.
(17) *We Also Served,* Page 79.
(18) Ibid, Page 78.
(19) Nicholson, Page 47.
(20) Derek E. Johnson: *East Anglia at War*, 1939-45.
(21) Collier, Pages 132-3.
(22) Roskill, Page 251.
(23) Mass Observation archive, personal diaries.
(24) "German bomber down in Suffolk", Mass Observation Report No 187.
(25) Regional Commissioners' Registered Files, Public Record Office, HO 207.
(26) Macleod and Kelly, Page 368.
(27) Collier, Page 144.

Chapter 7

Much detailed research has been done in the last few years on the Battle of Britain, including analysis of individual operations and the losses of planes and pilots. Francis K. Mason's *Battle over Britain* is a comprehensive and authoritative source-book, which has been supplemented in the compilation of this chapter by Winston Ramsey's *The Battle of Britain — Then and Now*.

(1) *Eastern Daily Press*, January 11th, 1940.
(2) Collier.
(3) R. J. Thompson: *Battle over Essex*.
(4) Mason, Pages 249-50.
(5) Fleming, Page 215.
(6) Quoted by Christopher R. Elliott, *East Anglian Magazine*, July 1969.
(7) Mason, Page 344.
(8) Collier, Page 216.
(9) Churchill, Volume 2, Pages 260-2.
(10) Collier, Page 144.

(11) Churchill, Page 257.
(12) "A.R.P. Material, 1939-45", Suffolk Record Office, Ipswich, HD 809.
(13) Ibid.
(14) Ibid.
(15) Fleming, Page 258, and Ramsey, Page 179.
(16) "Log Book of Hauxton Voluntary Defence Forces, 1940-1", Cambridgeshire Local History Collection, Cambridge.
(17) Norman Longmate: *How we lived then*, Page 111.
(18) Diary of John Allpress, made available by the author.

Chapter 8

The Mass Observation archive of material which was actually written during the summer of 1940 is the most valuable original source of information about this period, supplemented by the regional newspapers. Information about the financial problems of the east coast seaside resorts is contained in Home Office file "Coast towns finances" (HO 207/1155) at the Public Record Office, and about War Cabinet consideration of the problem in CAB 65/WM (40).

(1) R. J. Thompson: *Battle over Essex*.
(2) E. S. Turner: *The Phoney War on the Home Front*, Page 155.
(3) *East Anglian Magazine*, September 1965: Article by J. E. Siddall, former Town Clerk of Wisbech.
(4) Mass Observation archive, personal diaries.
(5) Churchill, Vol. 2., Page 151.
(6) O'Brien, Page 363.
(7) *Sunday Dispatch*, September 1st, 1940: Report by the Marquess of Donegall.
(8) "Morale in Coastal Suffolk", Mass Observation Report No 372.
(9) Home Office file, "Coast towns finances", Public Record Office, HO 207/1155.
(10) Ford Jenkins: *Lowestoft — Port War, 1939-45*.
(11) Paul Lund and Harry Ludlam: *Trawlers go to War*.
(12) Home Office file, "Coast towns finances", Public Record Office, HO 207/1155.

Chapter 9

Basic factual information about the course of the war in the later months of 1940 can be found in Basil Collier's *The Defence of the United Kingdom*, Captain S. W. Roskill's *The War at Sea*, and Francis K. Mason's *Battle over Britain*. Information about air raids on East Anglian towns comes from the locally-published accounts already mentioned.

(1) This description comes from the diary kept by John Allpress, then a young man living in Bury St Edmunds.
(2) Basil Collier: *A Short History of the Second World War*, Page 175.
(3) Ibid, Page 175.
(4) Trevor A. Bevis: *From out of the Sky — March and World War II*.
(5) Home Office leaflet No 5, *Fire precautions in war time*, 1939.
(6) Basil Collier: *The Defence of the United Kingdom*, Page 230.
(7) Ibid, Page 230.
(8) Nicholson: *The Suffolk Regiment*.
(9) Churchill, Vol. 2., Pages 620-1.
(10) Roskill, Page 327.
(11) Mass Observation archive, personal diaries.
(12) *Sunday Times*, January 25th 1981.
(13) *Cambridge Independent Press*, September 14th 1945; *Cambridge Evening News*, January 30th and February 15th, 1975.
(14) "A.R.P. Material, 1939-45", Suffolk Record Office, Ipswich, HD 809.

A Selected Bibliography

Volumes in the official History of the Second World War, published by H.M.S.O.:
  Basil Collier: *The Defence of the United Kingdom*, 1957.
  Terence H. O'Brien: *Civil Defence*, 1955.
  Richard M. Titmuss: *Problems of Social Policy*, 1950.
  Denis Richards: *The Royal Air Force*, Vol. 1. *The Fight at Odds*, 1953.
  Capt. S. W. Roskill, DSC, RN: *The War at Sea, 1939-45*, Vol 1., 1954.
Winston S. Churchill: *The Second World War*, Vol 1. *The Gathering Storm*, Cassell, 1948; and Vol 2. *Their Finest Hour*, Cassell, 1949.
A. J. P. Taylor: *English History, 1914-1945*, O.U.P., 1965.
Basil Collier: *A Short History of the Second World War*, Collins, 1967.
Roderick Macleod and Denis Kelly: *The Ironside Diaries, 1937-40*, Constable, 1962.
Charles Graves: *The Home Guard of Britain*, Hutchinson, 1943.
David Lampe: *The Last Ditch*, Cassell, 1968.
Dr R. V. Jones: *Most Secret War*, Hamish Hamilton, 1978.
Peter Fleming: *Invasion 1940*, Hamish Hamilton, 1958.
Francis K. Mason: *Battle over Britain*, McWhirter Twins Ltd, 1969.
Winston Ramsey: *The Battle of Britain — Then and Now*, After the Battle, 1980.
Angus Calder: *The People's War*, Cape, 1969.
Susan Briggs: *Keep Smiling Through*, Weidenfeld & Nicolson, 1975.
E. S. Turner: *The Phoney War on the Home Front*, Michael Joseph, 1961.
Norman Longmate: *How we lived then*, Hutchinson, 1971.
Leonard Mosley: *Backs to the Wall*, Weidenfeld & Nicolson, 1971.
Paul Lund and Harry Ludlam: *Trawlers go to War*, New English Library, 1972.
Robert Malster: *Saved from the Sea*, Dalton, 1974.
Michael J. F. Bowyer: *Action Stations — Wartime Military Airfields of East Anglia, 1939-45*, Patrick Stephens, 1979.
Col. W. N. Nicholson, CMG, DSO: *The Suffolk Regiment, 1928-46*, East Anglian Magazine, n.d.
Guthrie Moir: *The Suffolk Regiment*, Leo Cooper Ltd, 1969.
Tim Carew: *The Royal Norfolk Regiment*, Hamish Hamilton, 1967.
Col. T. A. Martin, MBE: *The Essex Regiment, 1929-50*, The Essex Regiment Association, 1952.
Cambridgeshire and Isle of Ely Territorial Army Association: *We Also Served, 1940-43*, Privately printed, Cambridge, 1944.
Derek E. Johnson: *East Anglia at War, 1939-45*, Jarrold, 1978.
Joan Banger: *Norwich at War*, Wensum Books, 1974.
Jeffrey Barham: *Cambridgeshire at War*, Birds Farm Publications, 1977.
Ford Jenkins: *Lowestoft — Port War, 1939-45*, W. S. Cowell, Ipswich, n.d.
R. J. Thompson: *Battle over Essex*, Essex Chronicle, n.d.
Norfolk County Council: *The War in Norfolk*, Report of the Chief Constable, 1945.
East Suffolk County Council: *Civil Defence in East Suffolk*, Ipswich, 1948.
Trevor A. Bevis: *From out of the Sky — March and World War II*, Westrydale Press, 1978.
Allan Jobson: *The Felixstowe Story*, Hale, 1968.
Leonard T. Weaver: *The Harwich Story*, Harwich Printing Co., 1945; and *The Borough of Harwich, 1318-1974*, Harwich Borough Council, 1974.
Harry Hitchman: *Harwich, the versatile seaport*, Published privately, 1975.
N. Scarfe: *The growth of Aldeburgh*, 1951.
Alexander Gow: *Letters from Cambridge*, Cape, 1945.
R. A. Whitehead: *Garrett 200 — a Bicentary History of Garretts of Leiston, 1778-1978*, Transport Bookman Publications, 1978.
Cambridgeshire Daily News, 1940. *Cambridge Review*, 1940. *Eastern Daily Press*, 1940. *East Anglian Daily Times*, 1940. *Essex County Standard*, 1940.

Index